AWS Certified SysOps Administrator - Associate

Practice Questions

Version 3

Document Control

Proposal Name   : AWS SysOps Admin Associate – Practice Questions

Document Version   : 3.0

Document Release Date : 5th Dec – 2019

Reference   : SOA-C01

Feedback:

If you have any comments regarding the quality of this book, or otherwise alter it to better suit your needs, you can contact us through email at info@ipspecialist.net

Please make sure to include the book's title and ISBN in your message.

About IPSpecialist

IPSPECIALIST LTD. IS COMMITTED TO EXCELLENCE AND DEDICATED TO YOUR SUCCESS.

Our philosophy is to treat our customers like family. We want you to succeed, and we are willing to do anything possible to help you make it happen. We have the proof to back up our claims. We strive to accelerate billions of careers with great courses, accessibility, and affordability. We believe that continuous learning and knowledge evolution are most important things to keep re-skilling and up-skilling the world.

Planning and creating a specific goal is where IPSpecialist helps. We can create a career track that suits your visions as well as develop the competencies you need to become a professional Network Engineer. We can also assist you with the execution and evaluation of proficiency level based on the career track you choose, as they are customized to fit your specific goals.

We help you STAND OUT from the crowd through our detailed IP training content packages.

Course Features:

❖ Self-Paced Learning
  • Learn at your own pace and in your own time
❖ Covers Complete Exam Blueprint
  • Prep-up for the exam with confidence
❖ Case Study Based Learning
  • Relate the content with real life scenarios
❖ Subscriptions that Suits You
  • Get more and pay less with IPS Subscriptions
❖ Career Advisory Services
  • Let industry experts plan your career journey
❖ Virtual Labs to test your skills
  • With IPS vRacks, you can evaluate your exam preparations
❖ Practice Questions
  • Practice Questions to assess your preparation standards
❖ On Request Digital Certification
  • On request digital certification from IPSpecialist LTD.

About the Authors:

This book has been compiled with the help of multiple professional engineers. These engineers specialize in different fields e.g., Networking, Security, Cloud, Big Data, IoT etc. Each engineer develops content in its specialized field that is compiled to form a comprehensive certification guide.

About the Technical Reviewers:

Nouman Ahmed Khan

AWS-Architect, CCDE, CCIEX5 (R&S, SP, Security, DC, Wireless), CISSP, CISA, CISM is a Solution Architect working with a major telecommunication provider in Qatar. He works with enterprises, mega-projects, and service providers to help them select the best-fit technology solutions. He also works closely as a consultant to understand customer business processes and help select an appropriate technology strategy to support business goals. He has more than fourteen years of experience working in Pakistan/Middle-East & UK. He holds a Bachelor of Engineering Degree from NED University, Pakistan, and M.Sc. in Computer Networks from the UK.

Abubakar Saeed

Abubakar Saeed has more than twenty-five years of experience, Managing, Consulting, Designing, and implementing large-scale technology projects, extensive experience heading ISP operations, solutions integration, heading Product Development, Presales, and Solution Design. Emphasizing on adhering to Project timelines and delivering as per customer expectations, he always leads the project in the right direction with his innovative ideas and excellent management.

Syed Hanif Wasti

Syed Hanif Wasti is a Computer Science graduate working professionally as a Technical Content Developer. He is a part of a team of professionals operating in the E-learning and digital education sector. He holds a Bachelor's Degree in Computer Sciences from PAF-KIET, Pakistan. He has completed training of MCP and CCNA. He has both technical knowledge and industry sounding information, which he uses efficiently in his career. He was working as a Database and Network administrator while having experience of software development.

Areeba Tanveer

Areeba Tanveer is an AWS Certified Solution Architect – Associate working professionally as a Technical Content Developer. She holds a Bachelor's of Engineering degree in Telecommunication Engineering from NED University of Engineering and Technology. She also worked as a project

Engineer in Pakistan Telecommunication Company Limited (PTCL). She has both the technical knowledge and industry sounding information, which she utilizes effectively when needed.

Muhammad Yousuf

Muhammad Yousuf is a professional technical content writer. He is a Certified Ethical Hacker (v10) and Cisco Certified Network Associate in Routing and Switching, holding a Bachelor's Degree in Telecommunication Engineering from Sir Syed University of Engineering and Technology. He has both technical knowledge and industry sounding information, which he uses perfectly in his career.

Free Resources:

With each workbook you buy from Amazon, IPSpecialist offers free resources to our valuable customers.

Once you buy this book, you will have to contact us at support@ipspecialist.net or tweet @ipspecialistoff to get this limited time offer without any extra charges.

Free Resources Include:

Exam Practice Questions in Quiz Simulation: With more than 250+ Q/A, IPSpecialist's Practice Questions is a concise collection of important topics to keep in mind. The questions are especially prepared following the exam blueprint to give you a clear understanding of what to expect from the certification exam. It goes further on to give answers with thorough explanations. In short, it is a perfect resource that helps you evaluate your preparation for the exam.

Career Report: This report is a step by step guide for a novice who wants to develop his/her career in the field of computer networks. It answers the following queries:
- What are the current scenarios and future prospects?
- Is this industry moving towards saturation or are new opportunities knocking at the door?
- What will the monetary benefits be?
- Why get certified?
- How to plan and when will I complete the certifications if I start today?
- Is there any career track that I can follow to accomplish specialization level?

Furthermore, this guide provides a comprehensive career path towards being a specialist in the field of networking and also highlights the tracks needed to obtain certification.

IPS Personalized Technical Support for Customers: Good customer service means helping customers efficiently, in a friendly manner. It is essential to be able to handle issues for customers and do your best to ensure they are satisfied. Providing good service is one of the most important things that can set our business apart from the others of its kind.

Great customer service will result in attracting more customers and attain maximum customer retention.

IPS is offering personalized TECH support to customers in order to provide better value for money. If you have any queries related to technology and labs you can simply ask our technical team for assistance via Live Chat or Email.

Our Products

Technology Workbooks

IPSpecialist Technology workbooks are the ideal guides to developing the hands-on skills necessary to pass the exam. Our workbook covers official exam blueprint and explains the technology with real life case study based labs. The contents covered in each workbook consist of individually focused technology topics presented in an easy-to-follow, goal-oriented, step-by-step approach. Every scenario features detailed breakdowns and thorough verifications to help you completely understand the task and associated technology.

We extensively used mind maps in our workbooks to visually explain the technology. Our workbooks have become a widely used tool to learn and remember the information effectively.

vRacks

Our highly scalable and innovative virtualized lab platforms let you practice the IP Specialist Technology Workbook at your own time and your own place as per your convenience.

Quick Reference Sheets

Our Quick Reference Sheets are a concise bundling of condensed notes of the complete exam blueprint. It is an ideal and handy document to help you remember the most important technology concepts related to certification exam.

Practice Questions

IP Specialists' Practice Questions are dedicatedly designed according to the certification exam perspective. The collection of these questions from our technology workbooks are prepared to keep the exam blueprint in mind, covering not only important but necessary topics as well. It is an ideal document to practice and revise for your certification.

AWS Certifications

AWS Certifications are industry-recognized credentials that validate your technical cloud skills and expertise while assisting you in your career growth. These are one of the most valuable IT certifications right now since AWS has established an overwhelming lead in the public cloud market. Even with the presence of several tough competitors such as Microsoft Azure, Google Cloud Engine, and Rackspace, AWS is by far the dominant public cloud platform today, with an astounding collection of proprietary services that continues to grow.

The two key reasons as to why AWS certifications are prevailing in the current cloud-oriented job market:

- There is a dire need for skilled cloud engineers, developers, and architects – and the current shortage of experts is expected to continue into the foreseeable future
- AWS certifications stand out for their thoroughness, rigor, consistency, and appropriateness for critical cloud engineering positions

Value of AWS Certifications

AWS places equal emphasis on sound conceptual knowledge of its entire platform, as well as on hands-on experience with the AWS infrastructure and its many unique and complex components and services.

For Individuals

- Demonstrate your expertise to design, deploy, and operate highly available, cost-effective, and secure applications on AWS
- Gain recognition and visibility for your proven skills and proficiency with AWS
- Earn tangible benefits such as access to the AWS Certified LinkedIn Community, invites to AWS Certification Appreciation Receptions and Lounges, AWS Certification Practice Exam Voucher, Digital Badge for certification validation, AWS Certified Logo usage, access to AWS Certified Store
- Foster credibility with your employer and peers

For Employers

- Identify skilled professionals to lead IT initiatives with AWS technologies
- Reduce risks and costs to implement your workloads and projects on the AWS platform
- Increase customer satisfaction

Types of Certification

Role-Based Certifications:

- **Foundational** - Validates overall understanding of the AWS Cloud. Prerequisite to achieving Specialty certification or an optional start towards Associate certification
- **Associate** - Technical role-based certifications. No prerequisite required
- **Professional** - Highest level technical role-based certification. Relevant Associate certification required

Specialty Certifications:

- Validate advanced skills in specific technical areas
- Require one active role-based certification

About AWS – Certified SysOps Administrator - Associate Exam

Exam Questions	Multiple Choice and Multiple Answer
Time to Complete	130 minutes
Available Languages	English, Japanese, Korean, and Simplified Chinese
Practice Exam Fee	20 USD
Exam Fee	150 USD

The AWS Certified SysOps Administrator – Associate exam validates the technical skills and experience of administrators in system operations role with at least one year of experience in deployment, management, and operations on AWS.

Example concepts you should understand for this exam include:

- ➢ Deployment, management, and operating of scalable, highly available, and fault-tolerant systems on AWS
- ➢ Implement and control the flow of data to and from AWS
- ➢ Selection of appropriate AWS services based on compute, data, or security requirements
- ➢ Identification of appropriate use of AWS operational best practices
- ➢ Estimation of AWS usage costs and identification of operational cost control mechanisms
- ➢ Migrate on-premises workloads to AWS

Recommended AWS Knowledge

- ➢ Understanding of the AWS tenets – architecting for the cloud
- ➢ Hands-on experience with the AWS CLI and SDKs/API tools
- ➢ Understanding of network technologies as they relate to AWS
- ➢ Understanding of security concepts with hands-on experience in implementing security controls and compliance requirements
- ➢ Understanding of virtualization technology
- ➢ Monitoring and auditing systems experience
- ➢ Knowledge of networking concepts (e.g., DNS, TCP/IP, and firewalls)
- ➢ Ability to translate architectural requirements

	Domain	% of Examination
Domain 1	Monitoring and Reporting	22%
Domain 2	High Availability	8%
Domain 3	Deployment & Provisioning	14%
Domain 4	Storage & Data Management	12%
Domain 5	Security & Compliance	18%
Domain 6	Networking	14%
Domain 7	Automation & Optimization	12%
Total		100%

Practice Questions

1. An organization plans to host databases on EC2 instances. What type of EBS volume should be used as the databases get heavy read/write activities?
   A. Cold HDD
   B. Provisioned IOPS
   C. General Purpose SSD
   D. Throughput optimized HDD

Answer: B

Explanation: Provisioned IOPS is the highest performance SSD that used is for high throughput workloads. It is mostly used for databases workloads.

2. An enterprise wants to back-up its EBS volumes. How would this be performed? (Choose 2)
   A. By enabling the replication flag on the EBS volumes
   B. By enabling Automated backups for EBS volumes
   C. By enabling volume copy for the EBS volumes
   D. By creating EBS Snapshots

Answer: B and D

Explanation: AWS Backup is a fully managed backup service, allowing you to centralize and automate data backup across AWS cloud services and locations via the AWS Storage Gateway. So you can integrate EBS with AWS backup to secure your volumes. You can also backup by taking a point in time snapshot of EBS volume, which is an incremental backup. This means that only the latest changes will be saved whenever changes are made on volume.

3. You plan on creating an AWS account on which a huge number of resources will be hosted. As an operation manager, you want to understand all the ways in which performance, cost and resource security can be improved. Which service would you use for this requirement?
   A. AWS CloudFront
   B. AWS WAF
   C. AWS Trusted Advisor
   D. AWS Inspector

Answer: C

Explanation: It is an online tool for real time guidance of provisioning the resources for improving the security, reducing the cost and increasing the performance.

4. To enhance safety, an enterprise has developed VPC endpoints for AWS Systems Manager access from a private subnet that is on a non-default VPC. In this VPC, managed EC2 instance has a user data script for the aws: domainJoin plugin. With AWS Systems Manager Patch Manager, instances are being patched with the latest security patches but cannot connect to the S3 buckets to store the patches. What measures can be taken to guarantee that the EC2 instance is successfully patched?
   A. Creating a VPC endpoint policy to provide access to S3 buckets used by Patch Manager
   B. Making sure the Security Group attached to VPC endpoint allows outgoing connections on port 443 from the private subnet
   C. Creating a VPC endpoint in a default VPC instead of non-default VPC
   D. Using public subnets for managed instance to access S3 buckets used by Patch Manager

Answer: A

Explanation: Patch Manager for AWS Systems Manager utilizes S3 buckets to store EC2 instance codes, which are updated while patching. When a VPC endpoint is created, its policy should allow access to the S3 buckets of the patch manager.

5. A company plans to transfer a large amount of information to S3 as they are using AWS for storage. The data is about 100 TB. What is the best way of transferring this amount of data?
   A. Setting up VPC Peering
   B. Setting up an AWS Direct Connect connection
   C. Using the Snowball device
   D. Setting up an AWS Managed VPN Connection

Answer: C

Explanation: For fast transfer of a huge amount of data, you can use AWS Snowball device. It is a physical device that bypasses the internet and transport data faster than the internet. You can transfer hundreds of terabytes or petabytes of information to Amazon Simple Storage Service (Amazon S3) using a Snowball.

6. A company wants to setup System Manager for 50 databases after a successful setup on EC2 in all regions. The databases are deployed in local a data center. What are the steps required for completing the installation of the System Manager on the database server? (Choose 4)

    A. Create a managed Instance activation for servers in Data Center
    B. Create an S3 bucket to store all Service Manager logs
    C. Setup a Direct Connect link between Data Center and VPC
    D. Install a TLS certificate on servers in Data Center
    E. Create an IAM role to communicate with the System Manager service
    F. Download and install SSM Agent on servers in Data Center
    G. Enable Advanced-instance tier

Answer: A, D, E and F

Explanation: Following measures need to be taken to establish a System Manager for the Hybrid environment:

   • The general setting of Systems Manager
   • IAM role for Hybrid Environment
   • For Hybrid Environment, create Managed-Instance activation
   • Install TLS certificate in on-premises servers and VMs
   • Install SSM agent

7. For storing critical information, an organization uses the Amazon S3 buckets. It needs a detailed log on all user access and the actions they performed on these S3 buckets. Now, the organization is planning to enable Amazon S3 server access logs for all these buckets. What are the permissions needed for the logs so that log files will be delivered to the destination bucket?

    A. Grant full permission to Log Delivery group on S3 Bucket "targetexample" using a bucket policy
    B. Grant full permission to Log Delivery group on S3 Bucket "targetexample" using bucket ACL
    C. Grant write permission to Log Delivery group on S3 Bucket "targetexample" using a bucket policy
    D. Grant write permission to Log Delivery group on S3 Bucket "targetexample" using bucket ACL

Answer: D

Explanation: Amazon S3 uploads access log files to target buckets using a special account, as Log Delivery group. As the log files need to be written, the account bucket must have write access defined by bucket ACL.

8. An enterprise wants to store its important documents for 5 to 6 years without any changes and decides to use Amazon S3 Glacier with Vault lock. To deny all users the ability to make changes, Vault Lock is initiated. What are the steps needed to be taken to complete Amazon S3 Glacier Vault lock policy?
   A. Initiate Complete Vault Lock operation within 24 hours using Lock ID generated during Initiate Vault Lock
   B. Initiate Complete Vault Lock operation within 24 hours using customized Lock ID as per security guidelines
   C. Initiate Complete Vault Lock operation within 12 hours using Lock ID generated during Initiate Vault Lock
   D. Initiate Complete Vault Lock operation within 12 hours using customized Lock ID as per security guidelines

Answer: A

Explanation: A Vault Lock policy can be used to lock vault for any future changes. Vault lock policy has two steps; First is Initiate Vault Lock, which is attaching a policy to the vault that returns unique lock ID. Second is Complete Vault Lock, which is required to be initiated within 24 hours otherwise, it expires.

9. A company has web application hosted on an EC2 instance placed behind a load balancer. In order to avoid any attack, the company requires security for its applications. To secure web applications, the security team regularly shares a number of blacklisted IP addresses and malicious SQL code that needs to be blocked. The monitoring team monitors traffic and instantly uses this filter to block attacks. How can the web application be safe against external attacks?
   A. By using AWS WAF to create a rate-based rule to deny IP address & SQL attacks on application
   B. By using AWS WAF to create a regular rule to deny IP address & SQL attacks on application
   C. By using AWS Shield Advanced to secure web-application
   D. By using AWS Shield Standard to secure web-application

Answer: B

Explanation: To block attacks on a web application with a customized solution, you can use AWS WAF. With AWS WAF, you can apply a rule to deny traffic to web applications. Attacks can be blocked by using cross site scripting, SQL injection, IP addresses, length request, string match etc.

10. A company performs some changes to its application. Currently, the application uses Route 53 as DNS service that is in a production environment. For a new application version, the company needs a separate environment on which testing needs to be performed. For testing, it needs a set of traffic directed toward this new version before the final shifting of all traffic towards it. How can this be done?

    A. 2 resource records based on the Weighted Routing Policy
    B. 1 resource record based on the Geo-Location Routing Policy
    C. 1 resource record based on the Latency Routing Policy
    D. 2 resource records based on the Simple Routing Policy

Answer: A

Explanation: Weighted routing allows you to connect multiple resources to a single domain name (for example: .com) or subdomain name (acme.example.com). For several purposes, this can be useful, including the balance of loads and the testing of new software versions.

11. A set of EC2 instances is launched, but goes into the terminated state after pending state. What was the reason behind this?

    A. The EBS snapshot from which the instance is being launched is corrupt
    B. You have reached the limit for EC2 instances in your region
    C. AWS does not have sufficient capacity
    D. You have reached the limit for EC2 instances in your region

Answer: A and B

Explanation: The following are the reasons for immediately terminating instances:.

- When you have reached to EBS volume limit
- When EBS snapshot is corrupt
- When EBS volume is encrypted, and you have no appropriate key permission to decrypt etc.

12. An enterprise is using S3 bucket for its application, and now it wants to get notified about API activities on this bucket. How can this requirement be fulfilled?
    A. By configuring CloudWatch metrics for S3
    B. By configuring CloudWatch agents for S3
    C. By configuring a Cloud Trail with SNS to send messages to the enterprise
    D. By configuring a CloudWatch log group for the API activity

Answer: C

Explanation: For monitoring API calls and getting notifications about the API activities, you can use Cloud Trail with SNS.

13. An organization wants a support plan for its critical applications on AWS that are the revenue generating applications. The company wants the support plan to have operational reviews and the response time of critical issue is to be 30 minutes or less. From the following, which support plan meets these requirements?
    A. Basic
    B. Business
    C. Developer
    D. Enterprise

Answer: D

Explanation: In "Enterprise" support plan, operational reviews are supported, you can even get reports as well. The response time for critical issues is <15 minutes while for production system down response time is <1 hour.

14. A company has a VPC, and in its private subnet, it has an EC2 instance on which application is deployed. Now, this instance needs to communicate with S3 service but is unable to do that. If the company are sure about the IAM permission that is assigned to the EC2 instance, then what is the issue behind this?
    A. The NACLs for the subnet is not allowing incoming traffic from S3
    B. A VPC gateway endpoint is not attached to the VPC
    C. The Security Groups for the EC2 Instances are not allowing incoming traffic from S3
    D. The S3 bucket does not have a well-defined bucket policy

Answer: B

Explanation: With the use of VPC endpoint, you can access the S3 resources from VPC. With this, you do not require any NAT instance or gateway. In order to allow an access to the bucket via a specific VPC or a VPC endpoint, define the bucket policy inside the bucket.

15. Which AWS service can an organization use for taking the log data of all resources in real-time and then scanning it for any sort of threats?

A. AWS Kinesis
B. AWS SQS
C. AWS Lambda
D. AWS SNS

Answer: A

Explanation: With Amazon Kinesis Data Streams, you can log real-time data and make it available for real-time analytics within milliseconds. It can capture the gigabytes of data from multiple resources.

16. A policy has been setup. What does this policy do?

```
{
  "Version": "2012-10-17",
  "Id": "S3PolicyId1",
  "Statement": [
    {
      "Sid": "IPAllow",
      "Effect": "Allow",
      "Principal": "*",
      "Action": "s3:*",
      "Resource": "arn:aws:s3:::ipsbucket/*",
      "Condition": {
        "IpAddress": {"aws:SourceIp": "10.20.140.0/24"},
        "NotIpAddress": {"aws:SourceIp": "10.20.140.188/32"}
      }
    }
  ]
}
```

A. Ensure that the client with the IP of 10.20.140.188 is allowed access to the objects in the demobucket

B. Ensure that clients in the range of 10.20.140.0/24 are denied access to all objects in the demobucket

C. Ensure that the client with the IP of 10.20.140.188 is denied access to the objects in the demobucket

D. Ensure that clients outside the range of 10.20.140.0/24 have access to all objects in the demobucket

Answer: C

Explanation: The above given conditions define that except IP: 10.20.140.188, all other IPv4 addresses from the range 10.20.140.0/24 have allowed access to S3 bucket.

17. An organization wants to set up multiple AWS accounts but with the condition that some services and actions are not allowed to all accounts. How can this be configured for their accounts?

A. By using AWS Organizations and Service Control Policies

B. By denying the services to be used across accounts by contact AWS

C. By creating an IAM policy per account and applying them accordingly

D. By creating a common IAM policy that can be applied across all accounts

Answer: A

Explanation: With AWS Organization, you can consolidate your all AWS account, and with Service Control policies, you have the benefit to define policies. In this policy, you specify resources and actions that users and roles in the accounts can use.

18. An enterprise plans to allow its admin to launch an EC2 instances that will be hosting applications and will need access to DynamoDB table. The administrator needs some permissions to meet the requirements, what are these? (Choose 2)

A. An IAM permission policy that allows the user to assume a role

B. An IAM permission policy that allows the user to pass a role

C. A trust policy that allows the user to assume a role

D. A trust policy that allows the EC2 Instance to assume a role

Answer: B and D

Explanation: Trust policy for the role allows the service to assume the role. You can attach the trust policy to the role. IAM permission policy that is attached to the IAM user allows the user to pass the role. These roles are approved to pass and the user can also view these roles details.

19. For its web application, a media company uses Convertible Reserved Instances. The company uses the detailed billing report for cost details but is planning to migrate to the AWS Cost & Usage Report. The AWS Cost & Usage Report is now compared with a detailed billing report in terms of changes by the admin. What is an important differentiator for the AWS Cost & Use Report?
    A. Multiple files with a fixed list of columns
    B. Single file with flexible column structure
    C. Multiple files with flexible column structure
    D. Single file with a fixed list of columns

Answer: C

Explanation: For all AWS resources, Cost & Usage report offers extensive cost information. We can also have custom reports with Cost & Usage. In this, there are multiple files including data files, separate files for discount and also the manifest file that lists the data files in report. You can add or delete columns from Cost & Usage reports on the basis of client demands.

20. Your company currently has a VPC with EC2 Instances. A new instance being launched will host an application that works on IPv6. To guarantee that the new instance communicates over IPv6, what should be the pre-conditions observed?
    A. Associate a NAT gateway to the VPC
    B. Ensure your VPC works in Dual stack mode
    C. Attach an egress-only internet gateway
    D. Associate a NAT Instance with the VPC

Answer: B

Explanation: You can enable IPv6 support for VPC and resources if you have existing VPCs, which support IPv4, and the resources in your subnet that are configured to use IPv4 only. Your VPC can work in dual-stack mode— it can interact through IPv4, IPv6, or both. Communication between IPv4 and IPv6 is mutually autonomous.

21. An organization is facing an issue in extending the storage on its on-premises infrastructure. The company wants the extension of the storage on AWS that will be available as iSCSI targets so that it can be referenced by the on-premises server. Which storage is used for this requirement?
    A. S3 storage
    B. EBS volume
    C. Storage Gateway Cached Volumes
    D. DynamoDB tables

Answer: C

Explanation: You can use S3 as primary storage and Storage Gateway Cached Volume as cached storage for the data that is frequently accessed locally. It gives low latency access to frequently accessed data. You can generate up to 32 tiB of storage volume and link it from your on-site app server as iSCSI devices. Your gateway stores the data you write in Amazon S3 for these amounts, maintains read data in your on-premises storage gateway's cache, and uploads buffer storage.

22. An enterprise had approximately 500 instances in AWS that are setup in a staging environment. Then the company moved to the production based instances. It wants SSH to always be disabled. What is the better way to assure that this security check is in place?
    A. Use AWS Config Rules to check the Security Groups
    B. Use the EC2 Config utility to check all the Security Groups
    C. Use the AWS Inspector to check the Security Groups
    D. Create a CLI script to check all the Security Groups

Answer: A

Explanation: You can check rules for any required condition. So make sure that the instances port 22 is not open in the production security group.

23. Your company has a large number of servers from which some of them are hosted in AWS and some are on-premises. Now, you want to monitor system level metrics of all server in a unified dashboard. Which of the following steps is needed to be taken for this requirement? (Choose 2)

A. Migrate the on-premises servers to AWS to ensure they can be monitored
B. Install the CloudWatch agent on both sets of servers
C. Setup the metrics dashboard in CloudWatch
D. Setup the metrics dashboard in CloudTrail

Answer: B and C

Explanation: As the requirement is unified monitoring, you can fulfill this requirement by installing CloudWatch agent on both side servers and then collecting system level metrics such as AWS or on-premises or hybrid environment. It also collects logs from both side servers as well.

24. An organization is using AWS CodeDeploy service for its application updates with a new password. The application updates are automated, but the company is concerned about the new password storage. How can it securely update its application password with less amount of effort and without any outage in the service?
A. By storing application password in EC2 instance
B. By storing application password in encrypted S3 Bucket & retrieving it while deploying
C. By using AWS CodeDeploy Source code to store application password
D. By using System Manager Parameter Store to store application password

Answer: D

Explanation: The parameter store of AWS Systems Manager provides a centralized store for saving configuration data in an encrypted format. Data can be referenced in the Parameter Store by AWS Services like AWS CodeDeploy, AWS Lambda & Amazon ECS. The Parameter Store enhances security by saving a password separately from the configuration files.

25. You are working as a SysOps Administrator for a large construction company. A few critical production servers were out of operation last week because an unauthorized third-party software has been installed on these servers. As a SysOps Administrator, you have been asked to maintain a pre-defined status for all instances in the US-West-1 region. What can be used to carry out this task?
A. State manager with Package Document
B. State manager with Command Document
C. State manager with Automation Document
D. State manager with Policy Document

Answer: B

Explanation: To keep EC2 in the pre-defined state, AWS Systems Manager uses State Manager with Package Documents. The Package document is used to create a zip folder, automation document is used for performing automation task, and a policy document is used to apply policy on instances.

26. On a Production S3 bucket, you have activated S3 server access logs. All S3 buckets are encrypted with SSE-KMS for safety reasons in the production environment. For logs, BucketSource is BucketA, and BucketB is the Target without prefixes. The critical files that are deleted from S3 buckets are done by IP address, so you need to find out the IP address of the requestor. No logs are generated after 4 hours in the target bucket. Which could be the reason that logs are not delivered in a selected bucket?

    A. The prefix in a BucketB needs to be specified while enabling logging
    B. Logs will be delivered in target bucket only after 24 hours of enabling logs
    C. BucketB has SSE-KMS encryption enabled that is not supported
    D. Source and target buckets are on a different bucket

Answer: C

Explanation: To deliver the logs in the target bucket, the bucket should be SSE-S3 encrypted and not SSE-KMS encrypted as it is not supported. However, when server access logs are enabled, within few hours, the delivery of logs to the target bucket will start

27. An enterprise has an AWS account that is actively being used. An external auditor carries out an audit. The auditor requires a user list, their status, to see whether MFA is used etc. How will you manage to get this list so you can give it to the auditor?

    A. By going to IAM and downloading the credential report
    B. By calling up AWS support to get the list of credentials
    C. By contacting an AWS partner to get the list of credentials
    D. By going to EC2 and downloading the credential report

Answer: A

Explanation: To download the report, you can use IAM API, Management console, CLI or AWS SDK. This credential contains a list of all users in an AWS Account along with the status of credentials, passwords, access key and MFA device.

28. A new VPC with a subnet has been configured. An Internet gateway has also been attached to the VPC. You made sure that the VPC allows DNS and hostname resolution. You launch an EC2 Instance with the public IP. The security groups and NACL are also set but still unable to connect to the instance. What should be taken as an extra step?

    A. Attach a NAT gateway to the VPC
    B. Ensure the Route table is modified
    C. Attach a Private IP to the Instance
    D. Add the Internet gateway to the subnet as well

Answer: B

Explanation: For internet access as in the question, everything is setup, but the route table has not been modified and this may be the reason behind not connecting to the instance.

29. An enterprise has a 3-tier application. The first layer is a presentation layer which is hosted in multiple webservers that are in public subnet. Second is an application layer that is hosted on 2 EC2 instances. The last layer is Oracle database servers that are hosted in EC2 instances and placed in the private subnet. You must make sure that all traffic is distributed equally. In addition, you must ensure that database servers are not internet accessible. What are the 2 configurations you needed to implement in order to meet the following requirement?

    A. Create an internal load balancer for the Database Layer
    B. Create an external load balancer for the web servers
    C. Create an external load balancer for the database servers
    D. Create an Internal load balancer for the web servers

Answer: A and B

Explanation: You can create an architecture that utilizes both internal and internet load balancers if your application has a multi-layer application, such as web servers that must be attached to the internet and database servers that can only be attached to web servers. So, create and register the web servers with an internet-facing load balancer. Create and register the database servers with an internal load balancer.

30. You have a VPC with EC2 Instances. A new instance will be introduced to host an IPv6 request. This instance must guarantee that you can initiate traffic to the Internet. Simultaneously, you must guarantee that no incoming internet connection to the instance is initiated. What would you include in the VPC?
    A. NAT gateway
    B. Internet gateway
    C. NAT instance
    D. An egress only gateway

Answer: D

Explanation: IPv6 addresses are unique globally, so they are public by default. As you want to prevent initiation of request from the internet to the instance but want an instance to access the internet then you can use Egress only Gateway.

31. An organization uses VPC Flow Logs to capture the IP traffic of the instance in VPC. The VPC Flow Logs writes multiple logs files on a single S3 bucket but only a few files are published to the encrypted S3 bucket. Later, when the subsequent log files were sent to be published, they failed. The organization got an error of permission "LogDestinationPermissionIssueException". How can this issue be handled?
    A. By granting permission to entire the bucket using arn:aws:s3:::bucket_name/*
    B. By making sure IAM user has permission to publish flow logs to an entire S3 bucket
    C. By creating a new log file to publish logs to S3 bucket since the existing log file size is greater than 75 Mb
    D. By adding a CMK Key as server-side encryption that is used for S3 buckets

Answer: A

Explanation: The policies of Amazon S3 Bucket are only 20 KB. If more than one flow log is directed at a single Amazon S3 bucket, it causes the bucket policy limit to be exceeded, which leads to an error. To fix this error, you can either delete unwanted flow logs or grant permission to the whole bucket via arn:aws:s3:bucketname/*. By adding this policy to bucket policies, the bucket policy will not exceed the limit.

32. You have a data center on AWS and on-premises. You are planning to use AWS Direct Connect to connect your data centers. What are the pre-requisite that are needed to be taken for this connection? (Choose 2)
    A. The network device on your side must support BGP
    B. The network device on your side must support static routing
    C. The network must use a dual mode fiber with a 1000BASE-LX
    D. The network must use a single mode fiber with a 1000BASE-LX

Answer: A and D

Explanation: The network requirements for AWS Direct Connect are:

- For 1 gigabit Ethernet, use single–mode fibre with a 1000BASE-LX (1310nm) transceiver

- For 10 gigabit Ethernet, use 10GBASE-LR (1310nm)

- Must support Border Gateway Protocol (BGP) and BGP MD5 authentications

- Across entire connection, 802.1Q VLAN must be supported

- Auto negotiation must be disabled for the port

33. In a CloudFormation template, which part of the template can you use to make it more dynamic in nature, so you can pass values in runtime?
    A. Outputs
    B. Parameters
    C. Conditions
    D. Mappings

Answer: B

Explanation: To pass a value to the template in runtime, you should refer to the Parameter part from resource and output section. Output is used to describe the value that are returned when you view stack property, while Condition contains statements that define the circumstances under which entities are created or configured. The Mappings section matches a key to a corresponding set of named values.

34. An institution wants to produce interactive dashboards for the evaluation of its new product. A financial institution is looking for a strong BI tool. For this necessity, the institution has

chosen Amazon QuickSight. When using Amazon QuickSight, which of these should be taken into account when selecting different editions? (Choose 3)

A. With Standard edition, you can select AD groups in directory services for access to Amazon QuickSight

B. Standard Edition does not support encryption at rest, while Enterprise edition supports encryption at rest

C. Enterprise Edition does not support encryption at rest, while Standard edition supports encryption at rest

D. With Standard edition, you can invite an IAM user & allow to use their credentials to access Amazon QuickSight

E. With Enterprise edition, you can invite an IAM user & allow to use their credentials to access Amazon QuickSight

F. With Enterprise edition, you can select AD groups in directory services for access to Amazon QuickSight

Answer: B, D and F

Explanation: Two editions are available in Amazon QuickSight: Standard & Enterprise Management Edition. You can invite IAM users to provide Amazon QuickSight access in Standard Edition. You need to pick AD Active Directory Group from AWS Directory Services in the Enterprise edition in order to provide administrative access to Amazon QuickSight. Enterprise edition also offers encryption at rest.

35. Multiple EC2 instances are running and for monitoring, a dashboard is needed. The dashboard should show CPU utilization metrics after every one-minute interval for all instances. What is a cost effective and easy way to get a dashboard? (Choose 2)

A. Create a dashboard in CloudWatch

B. Create a dashboard in CloudTrail

C. Enable detailed monitoring for the EC2 Instances

D. Enable basic monitoring for the EC2 Instances so that costs are kept in check

Answer: A and C

Explanation: When you launch an EC2 instance, it starts sending metrics to the CloudWatch. By default, this monitoring covers previous 5-minute activity. For every one-minute activity monitoring, you need to enable detailed monitoring. Via Cloud Watch dashboard, you can view monitoring of resource that is spread all over the region. With this, you can also create customized metrics of the resource.

36. For a big financial, you work as a SysOps administrator. The organization is using AWS EC2 instances for its extranet apps. Management has chosen to automate vulnerability checks to improve the safety of these Linux-based instances. You evaluate multiple methods to install Amazon Inspector on these instances, which is continually launched in large amount depending on customer demand. The security team has a mandate that this installation method does not require extra agents. What would assist install Amazon Inspector in the safest and least effort automatically?
    A. Use EC2 User Data Feature to install Amazon Inspector using the script
    B. Use Amazon EC2 Systems Manager Run Command to install Amazon Inspector
    C. Use Amazon Linux AMI with Amazon Inspector
    D. Use CloudWatch Events to trigger Lambda function that will run Amazon EC2 Systems Manager to install Amazon Inspector

Answer: C

Explanation: Amazon Marketplace has Amazon Linux AMI with an integrated Amazon Inspector agent that can be used on multiple EC2 instances to conduct vulnerability inspections.

37. A website is hosted in S3. It is required that when users access the website from no matter which part of the world, they get a seamless experience. How would you fulfill this requirement?
    A. By placing an Elastic Load balancer in front of the static web site
    B. By creating a Cloud Front distribution and place the S3 bucket as the source
    C. By enabling cross region replication for the web site in the S3 bucket
    D. By using ElastiCache to cache the Reponses

Answer: B

Explanation: Amazon CloudFront is a worldwide service (CDN) that provides secure, low latency, high transmission rate for delivering data, videos, apps, and APIs for viewers. CloudFront is built into AWS–including physical sites that are directly attached to the worldwide AWS infrastructure, as well as software that operates seamlessly on services such as AWS Sheild with DDoS Mitigation, Amazon S3, Elastic Load Balancing and Amazon EC2.

38. A company uses AWS to deploy its application on EC2 instance that sits behind an ELB. Now, the company wants a list of all client IPs who access the load balancer. How can this be done? (Choose 2)
    A. By giving access to the S3 bucket for accessing the logs
    B. By giving access to CloudWatch logs for accessing the logs
    C. By enabling access logging for the ELB
    D. By enabling CloudWatch logs for the individual EC2 Instances

Answer: A and C

Explanation: ELB offers access logs that give detailed information about the requests for a load balancer. These logs include the client IPs, request path, latencies, the time when request received etc. This access log feature is disabled by default and you need to enable it.

39. An institute has its network in AWS VPC and on-premises. For its hybrid network connectivity, the institute is planning to setup AWS VPN. How will this be implemented? (Choose 3)
    A. By attaching a virtual private gateway to the VPC
    B. By creating the VPN connection
    C. By ensuring that a customer gateway is in place
    D. By attaching an internet gateway to the VPC

Answer: A, B and C

Explanation: For creating a site to site VPN, you have to take the following steps:
- Create customer gateway
- Create a virtual private gateway
- Enable route propagation
- Modify security group
- Create a site to site VPN and configure customer gateway device

40. If an enterprise has instances in private subnet of VPC and these instance wants to download patch updates from the internet. No connection from the internet is origination to the instances. Also, they want that less amount of bandwidth restriction. How can they setup all this requirement?
    A. A NAT Instance setup in the public subnet
    B. An internet gateway attached to the VPC
    C. A NAT gateway setup in the public subnet

D. A NAT Instance setup in the private subnet

Answer: C

Explanation: You can use a Network Address Translation (NAT) gateway to allow instances in a private subnet to connect to the internet or other AWS services. However, it prevents the initiation of a connection from the internet.

41. Your company has a number of EC2 instances that would host manufacturing applications. The applications would run 24*7 around the clock, the entire year. During this period, you might need to upgrade the instance type as workloads are likely to change and as per needs, you should adapt. Which one is the most affordable price option for the instances?
    A. Convertible Reserved Instances
    B. On-Demand Instances
    C. Spot Instances
    D. Standard Reserved Instances

Answer: A

Explanation: You can use on-demand instances for temporary workloads and for batch processing, you can use spot instances. With Convertible Reserved Instances, you can change the instance family, type, platform, scope and tenancy. In Standard Reserved Instances, you cannot change the instance family, but you can change the size.

42. An enterprise needs to create a template in CloudFormation. In this template, it plans to launch EC2 instances and install application packages. Now, the enterprise wants that time stack should be successful only after a successful installation of software in the stack. How will this be done?
    A. By using CloudTrail to signal the completion
    B. By using CloudWatch logs to signal the completion
    C. By using the Change sets feature
    D. By using the cfn-signal helper script

Answer: D

Explanation: With cfn-signal helper script, you can give signal to AWS CloudFormation, about the successful creation and update of EC2 instance. You can also signal AWS CloudFormation about software applications that are ready after being installed and configured on the instances.

43. You work as a system administrator for a company. You have just provisioned a fleet of EC2 instances and realized that none of them has a public IP address. What are the settings for the next fleet of instances with public IP addresses that need to be changed?
    A. Modify the auto-assign public IP setting on the route table
    B. Modify the auto-assign public IP setting on the subnet
    C. Modify the auto-assign public IP setting on the VPC
    D. Modify the auto-assign public IP setting on the instance type

Answer: B

Explanation: To assign a public IP address to the instance, you have to perform auto assign public IP setting at subnet level by marking it true, which by default is false. This will assign a public IP to all the instances.

44. A company has custom a VPC in which they launched an EC2 instance inside a subnet. However, the instance is not getting public DNS Name. How can the company resolve this issue? (Choose 2)
    A. By ensuring the instance is launched with the right AMI
    B. By ensuring the instance is launched with the right EBS volume type
    C. By checking the enableDnsHostnames setting
    D. By checking the enableDnsSupport setting

Answer: C and D

Explanation: To ensure that the instance launched inside VPC receives Public DNS Name, you have 2 attributes inside VPC; enableDnsHostnames (Specifies that public IP address instances receive respective hostnames from the public DNS) and enableDnsSupport (Shows whether DNS resolution is supported). Instances in the VPC get public DNS-hostnames if "enableDnsHostname" attribute is true, in addition to this, "enableDnsSupport" attribute also needs to be true.

If both attributes are true, then instance with public IP start receiving the public DNS host name and Amazon-provided DNS server can resolve Amazon-provided private DNS hostnames.

45. An organization has a batch processing application that needs to be hosted on instances. You know that your application can be interrupted at any moment, and then resume by itself. You, as a system manager, need to provision EC2 instances with minimum cost. How would you do this?

A. Reserved Instances
B. Spot Instances
C. On-demand Instances
D. Dedicated Instances

Answer: B

Explanation: If your running application is interrupted, then spot instances are the most cost effective solution for the instances on which application is running. The applications are batch job, background processing, and data analyzing.

46. You are planning to use a database that contains critical information and needs to be fault tolerant. This database is hosted on an EC2 instance. If you plan to apply RAID configuration, then what implementation can you choose?

A. RAID 0
B. RAID 5
C. RAID 1
D. RAID 6

Answer: C

Explanation: When fault tolerance is more important than I/O performance, you can implement RAID 1. With this configuration, the data durability is increased. Amazon EBS is not recommended for RAID 5 and RAID 6 because some of the IOPS available in your volumes are consumed for parity writing of the RAID mode. These RAID modes offer 20-30 percent less usable IOPS than the RAID 0 setup, depending on the setup of your RAID array. In addition, higher expenses are a factor in these RAID modes. RAID 0 2 volume array can perform more than a RAID 6 4 volume array, which costs twice as much when using equal volume sizes and speeds.

47. A company develops an app that is hosted on AWS. The app must send messages across application components. The company needs to maintain the order of messages. Which of the following would provide this?

A. FIFO SQS Queue
B. Kinesis Streams
C. SNS Topic
D. Standard SQS Queue

Answer: A

Explanation: The FIFO queues are intended to enhance messages between applications when the sequence of operations and events are critical, or where duplicates cannot be tolerated.

48. You are using AWS resources currently, and want a data store for storing your historical data. This data needs to be queried by in-house built-in BI solution. From the following which storage is the best option?

A. AWS EBS
B. AWS DynamoDB
C. AWS Redshift
D. AWS EMR

Answer: C

Explanation: Amazon Redshift is a cloud data warehouse service that is fully managed and can scale up to petabyte. It is possible to begin with only a few hundred gigabytes and scale to a petabyte or more. This allows you to use your information to obtain new insights for your company and its clients.

The first step is to launch the Amazon Redshift cluster, which is a set of nodes. You can upload your data and then conduct data analysis queries. No matter the size of your information, Amazon Redshift provides high-performance querying.

49. A company has a VPC in which web application servers are deployed, and plan to update the security policy of instances. But because of manual error outage, the company needs some preventive measures. So, it wants to create a process for the evaluation of security policies post deployment. Which of the following measures is sufficient to evaluate network exposure to post changes to the security group efficiently?

A. Adding a CloudWatch Event rule to automatically trigger Network Assessment post changes in Security Groups
B. Installing an Amazon Inspector Agent on EC2 instance launched in a VPC to evaluate Security Groups
C. Initiating a network connection between EC2 instance to any destination outside VPC & use VPC Flow logs to evaluate open ports with Security Group
D. Installing third-party Network Port Scanning Tool on EC2 instance launched in a VPC

Answer: A

Explanation: The Amazon Inspector has network accessibility package that supports the evaluation of network settings that can be used in VPC to detect potential risk. This product does not need installation of Amazon inspector agent on an EC2 instance. For automation of assessments checks, CloudWatch event is used, which tracks Security Group modifications and initiates network assessments via the Network Reachability Package.

50. A pharmaceutical company plans to use AWS to host a three-stage web application. The company has several accounts based on vertical operations across regions. It now plans to build an AWS Organization for consolidated billing, for which it developed a master account. Which characteristics should be connected with a Master Account? (Choose 3)

A. A Master Account of an organization can be granted permission using service control policies
B. Pay all charges accrued by all the accounts in its organizational unit
C. Pay all charges accrued by all the accounts in its organization
D. Any Member Account can be upgraded to Master Account
E. Invite an external account to join your organization
F. Create an organization & organizational unit

Answer: C, E and F

Explanation: An organization and organizational unit can be created by a Master Account. They can also invite other accounts to enter their organization and be liable for all account fees.

51. A company has set up a set of EC2 instances in a VPC. For security analysis, the IT security department needs to view the IP address of incoming traffic. Which one of the following can help in this necessity?

A. AWS Inspector
B. AWS VPC Flow Logs
C. AWS CloudTrail logs
D. AWS Trusted Advisor

Answer: B

Explanation: VPC Flow Logs allows you to collect IP traffic information on your VPC to and from the network interfaces. Amazon CloudWatch Logs and Amazon S3 are then used to publish flow log information. You can recover and display the information in the selected location after creating a flow log.

52. An organization has set up a VPC in which it plans to install EC2 Instances. The instances will be included in a custom domain. Now, the organization needs the custom domain to not be accessible from the public internet but from the instances in VPC. How can this be done?
   A. By setting up a public hosted zone in Route 53
   B. By mentioning the custom domain in the DNS Resolution section
   C. By mentioning the custom domain name when creating the VPC
   D. By setting up a private hosted zone in Route 53

Answer: D

Explanation: A private host zone is a container which contains information on how the Amazon Route 53 is designed to address a domain and its subdomains, DNS queries within one or more VPCs that are created with VPC service.

53. A company uses EC2 instances on which Memcached is hosted. This will be used as cache service for its applications. What type of instance will you, as a system administrator, provision the instances with?
   A. Storage Optimized
   B. General Purpose
   C. Memory Optimized
   D. Compute Optimized

Answer: C

Explanation: Memory optimized instances are intended for delivering the fast performance of the workloads, which is for processing big information sets in memory. Memory optimized instance type is suitable for: relation databases that have high performance, for web scale caching, in-memory databases, HPC and EDA applications etc.

54. A company is using Service Control Policy (SCP), which is implemented at the level of the Organization Unit (OU) when using KMS in an AWS organization to improve security.

```
{
  "Version": "2012-10-17",
  "Statement": [
    {
      "Sid": "KMS"
      "Effect": "Deny",
      "Action": "kms:ScheduleKeyDeletion",
      "Resource": "*"
    }
  ]
}
```

From the following options, which one explains the policy in a proper way?

- A. This will deny users & roles in root accounts within all OUs in your organization to schedule a CMK deletion
- B. This will deny users & roles in all accounts within that OU to schedule a CMK deletion
- C. This will deny users & roles in all accounts within all OUs in your organization to schedule a CMK deletion
- D. This will deny users & roles in root accounts within that OUs to schedule a CMK deletion

Answer: B

Explanation: The Service Control Policy (SCP) allows for the setting of policies to control all accounts within organizations. It provides a list of actions that can be taken within an organization by an account. Since SCP is used at the OU level, the scenario above affects all accounts within the OU.

55. As an administrator, you manage the migration of application servers from on-premises to AWS. EC2 instances are launched by the developers to test application in the cloud. The

number of EC2 instances that are set up concerns you. Which service can be used to determine whether EC2 Instance numbers are within the relevant limits?

A. AWS Trusted Advisor
B. AWS Config
C. AWS CloudWatch
D. AWS System Manager

Answer: A

Explanation: To check usage detail in order to identify that specific resource is in service limit or not, you can use AWS Trusted Advisor.

56. An enterprise uses EC2 instance to host its application in AWS. Route 53 maps the IP of this instance to a custom domain. Which of the following should ideally be done for the instance, as an important execution step?

A. Ensure the instance is launched with Enhanced Networking
B. Ensure that the instance is associated with an Elastic IP
C. Ensure that the instance is created with an instance store AMI
D. Ensure that the instance is created with a public IP

Answer: B

Explanation: Ensure the instance starts with an Elastic IP in order to make sure that the IP address is not changed for that instance when the instance is stopped and restarted. An elastic IP address is a dynamic cloud-computing, static IPv4 address. Your AWS account is assigned to an Elastic IP address. You can mask an instance or software's failure by quickly remapping your address to another instance in your account with an Elastic IP address.

57. The EC2 Instances of your company are laid out. The company's IT Security has requested that the recent security patches should be added to every EC2 instance. Which of these can be used to ensure that this requirement is met?

A. AWS Trusted Advisor
B. AWS Config
C. AWS CloudWatch
D. AWS System Manager

Answer: D

Explanation: AWS Systems Manager Patch Manager automates the process of patching managed instances with security-related updates. You can also install patches for non-security updates for Linux instances. Amazon EC2 instances or on-site servers and Virtual Machines (VMs) can be patched according to their operating system type. Supporting versions for OS are Windows, Ubuntu Server, Red Hat Enterprise Linux (RHEL), SUSE Linux Enterprise Server (SLES) and Amazon Linux 2. You can only see a report on missing patches by scanning instances, or you can scan and install all missing patches automatically.

58. A financial institute has a fleet of EC2 instances that belongs to different departments. Now, the institute wants a report on the monthly cost of instances that will be department wise. How will this requirement be fulfilled?
    A. By using different AMI types for the underlying EC2 Instances
    B. By creating different VPCs for the EC2 Instances based on the departments
    C. By assigning tags to the EC2 Instances and generating reports based on the tags
    D. By creating different subnets for the EC2 Instances based on the departments

Answer: C

Explanation: You can use tags to organize your AWS bill to reflect your own cost structure. To do this, sign up to get your AWS account bill with tag key values included. To see the cost of your combined resources, you can organize your billing information based on resources that have the same tag key values. For example, you can tag several resources with a specific application name, and then organize your billing information to see the total cost of that application across several services.

59. A company is using AWS RDS MySQL database. It is facing some performance issue in the database and needs a way to improve its performance. How could this be done?
    A. AWS Performance Insights
    B. AWS Config
    C. AWS Trusted Advisor
    D. AWS Inspector

Answer: A

Explanation: Performance Insights extends current monitoring feature in Amazon RDS to demonstrate the efficiency of your database and assist you in evaluating any problems. You can

view the database load and filter the load via waits, SQL statements, hosts or users using the Performance Insights dashboard. For the DB instance, if you have more than one database, performance data for all databases are aggregated.

60. An organization want to encrypt all data store in S3 at rest. How is this possible?
   A. By using Server-side certificates to encrypt the objects at rest
   B. By using AWS server-side encryption for the S3 bucket with AWS S3 Managed Keys
   C. By using AWS server-side encryption for the S3 bucket with AWS KMS Keys
   D. By enabling SSL while accessing objects in the bucket

Answer: B and C

Explanation: If you want to encrypt data at rest, then use server side encryption. There are 3 types of server side encryption:

- Server-Side Encryption with Amazon S3-Managed Keys (SSE-S3)
- Server-Side Encryption with Keys Stored in AWS KMS (SSE-KMS)
- Server-Side Encryption with Customer-Provided Keys (SSE-C)

61. In the given policy, which permission is granted? (Choose 2)

```
{
    "Version": "2012-10-17",
    "Statement": [
        {
            "Sid": "ListObjectsInBucket",
            "Effect": "Allow",
            "Action": ["s3:ListBucket"],
            "Resource": ["arn:aws:s3:::ips"]
        },
        {
            "Sid": "AllObjectActions",
            "Effect": "Allow",
            "Action": "s3:*Object",
            "Resource": ["arn:aws:s3:::ips/*"]
        }
    ]
```

```
}
```

A. Read an object from the ips
B. Delete any object from the ips
C. Add an object to the ips
D. Add an object to any bucket

Answer: A and C

Explanation: This policy allows to read and write the operation of an object to the specific bucket. This policy permits only AWS APIs or AWS CLIs, and both are essential to complete this action.

62. A CIDR block of 10.0.0.0/16 has been setup for a VPC. The CIDR blocks 10.0.1.0/24 and 10.0.2.0/24 have been set up for the public and private subnet respectively. Also, an internet gateway to the VPC has been attached. In order to allow internet connectivity, which of these modifications must be made to the customized route table for a public subnet?

A. Add a Route entry of Destination of 10.0.2.0/16 and the Target as the internet gateway
B. Add a Route entry of Destination of 10.0.0.0/16 and the Target as the internet gateway
C. Add a Route entry of Destination of 0.0.0.0/0 and the Target as the internet gateway
D. Add a Route entry of Destination of 10.0.1.0/16 and the Target as the internet gateway

Answer: C

Explanation: For internet gateway connectivity, you need to add a route 0.0.0.0/0 in the route table.

63. A set of EC2 instances are placed in the public subnet of VPC. Now, the company observes that some malicious traffic is coming from a group of IP addresses and wants to block them. How would this be done?

A. Block the outgoing traffic using the NACL's for the subnets
B. Block the incoming traffic using the NACL's for the subnets
C. Block the outgoing traffic using the Security Groups for the EC2 Instances
D. Block the incoming traffic using the Security Groups for the EC2 Instances

Answer: B

Explanation: An ACL is an optional security layer for your VPC, acting as a traffic firewall within and out of one or more subnets. You can configure network ACLs with security group-similar rules to add an additional safety layer to the VPC.

64. You have three VPCs (VPC A, VPC B and VPC C) in your organization. All instances of all VPCs need to be able to interact with each other. You must make sure you have the required minimum settings to do so. What would you execute from the following steps? (Choose 2)

A. Ensure that the route tables only in VPC A and VPC B are updated with the respective peering configuration

B. Ensure that all route tables in each VPC are updated with the respective peering configuration

C. VPC A peered with VPC B, and VPC B peered with VPC C

D. VPC A peered with VPC B, and VPC A peered with VPC C, and VPC B peered with VPC C

Answer: B and D

Explanation: You have peered three VPCs together in a full mesh configuration. So, peer VPC A with VPC B and VPC A with VPC C then peer VPC B with VPC C. After peering, modify each route table with their respective peering configuration.

65. A company is using Lambda function, and now has updated the function so that it can access the DynamoDB tables. What changes should be made in order to perform certain actions?

A. Ensure the IAM role attached to the function has DynamoDB access

B. Change the log group assigned for the Lambda function

C. Change the memory assigned for the Lambda function

D. Change the Security Groups for the Lambda function

Answer: A

Explanation: No matter what invokes a Lambda function, a lambda function is executed by AWS Lambda on your behalf. You have to give the relevant permissions for accessing resources to your Lambda function. You must also allow AWS Lambda to view your DynamoDB stream. All permissions are granted in an IAM role that Lambda takes to poll streams and execute Lambda function.

66. In the recent AWS infrastructure, a large, multinational company has deployed web servers in EC2. This company administrator is looking to authenticate users using existing ADs to access

the EC2 instance deployed in AWS. What is the correct series of actions to ensure that the authentication is successful?

A. User is provided temporary credential by Identity Provider using Web Identity. Based upon this, user is authenticated with AD & provided access to AWS management console for 1 hour

B. User is authenticated by AD. Based upon group membership, Identity Provider forwards Web Identity response to AWS STS. Using STS AssumeRoleWithWebIdentity, the user is provided with a temporary credential for max 1 hour to access the AWS management console

C. User is authenticated by AD. Based upon group membership, Identity Provider forwards SAML response to AWS STS. Using STS AssumeRoleWithSAML, the user is provided with a temporary credential for max 1 hour to access the AWS management console

D. User is provided temporary credential by Identity Provider using SAML. Based upon this, user is authenticated with AD & provided access to the AWS management console for 1 hour

Answer: C

Explanation: The following steps are taken for authentication when using IAM Federated Sign-in with AD:

- Users access single sign-on page provided by Active Directory Federated Service & provide login credentials
- Active Directory Federated Service authenticates these users based upon Active Directory credentials
- Active Directory forwards users group membership
- Active Directory Federated Service uses this group membership information & creates SAML redirection link to forward to AWS STS
- AWS STS uses AssumeRoleWithSAML to grant temporary credentials to the user, which is valid for max 1 hour
- Users use this temporary credential to gain access to the AWS Management Console

67. An enterprise has a server on AWS and on-premises. It wants to get all the information on these servers like the types of software installed. This information will be stored in the management database. How will this be done?
    A. By using Amazon CloudWatch to get the configuration of all the servers
    B. By using the EC2 dashboard to get the configuration of all the servers
    C. By using the AWS Config tool to get the configuration of all the servers

D. By using the AWS Systems Manager to get the software inventory on the servers

Answer: D

Explanation: You can collect metadata, OS and applications from your Amazon EC2 instances as well as on-site or virtual (VM) servers in the hybrid network via AWS Systems Manager Inventory. You can quickly query the metadata to find out what instances running, what software, and what configurations need to do as per policy as well as what instances need updates.

68. An organization's development team currently has an application deployed on its on-premises environment. This application makes use of Docker containers. This environment must be shifted to AWS. The development team does not want the basic infrastructure to be managed. What is the ideal service should use to provide them with the environment?

A. AWS OpsWorks
B. AWS EC2
C. AWS Elastic Beanstalk
D. AWS CloudFormation

Answer: C

Explanation: Elastic Beanstalk supports the use of Docker container web applications. You can set your own runtime environment using Docker containers. You can choose your own platform, programming language and any applications that are not supported by other platforms such as package managers or tools. Docker containers are self-contained and include all settings and software that your web application needs to operate. By using Docker with Elastic Beanstalk, you have an infrastructure that handles the details of provisioning capacity, load balance, scaling and application health monitoring automatically.

69. You have a Linux based instance in default VPC and now you want to access this instance via keys. How will you do this?

A. The public key needs to be created and placed on the EC2 Instance
B. The private key needs to be used for logging into the instance
C. The private key needs to be created and placed on the EC2 Instance
D. The public key needs to be used for logging into the instance

Answer: A and B

Explanation: For logging into your instance, a key pair needs to be created, when you initiate the instance, you need to specify the key pair's name, and when you connect to the instance, you need to enter the private key. On a Linux instance, the public key content is placed in an entry within ~/.ssh/authorized_keys. This is done at boot time and allows you to securely use your private key instead of a password to access your instance.

70. A financial sector has a set of instances, for which they need to generate memory usage reports as its Admin wants to view the dashboards continuously. What steps do you need to take in order to meet this requirement?
    A. Use EC2 console to get the details
    B. Use CloudTrail logs for logging all the metrics
    C. Ensure that the EC2 Instance Config tool is installed on the Linux instance
    D. Ensure that the CloudWatch monitoring scripts are installed on the Linux Instances

Answer: D

Explanation: A new CloudWatch agent is available for multiple platforms. You can use a single agent to collect system measurements as well as log files from instances and servers of Amazon EC2 on-site. The new agent supports both Windows Server and Linux and allows you to choose the collected metrics, including metrics from the sub-resource, such as the CPU core. We suggest that you use the new agent to collect metrics and logs rather than old monitoring scripts.

71. The Chef Tool is currently used by a company to manage its underlying servers' configuration. You want to begin delivering servers in AWS Cloud. The company wants to ensure that it can use its existing Chef's configuration management recipes again. What service would you recommend from the following list to meet this requirement?
    A. AWS OpsWorks
    B. AWS EC2
    C. AWS CloudFormation
    D. AWS Elastic Beanstalk

Answer: A

Explanation: AWS OpsWorks is a configuration management service that can be used in a cloud company to set up and operate apps via Puppet or Chef. AWS OpsWorks stacks and AWS OpsWorks for Chef Automates enable you to use Chef cookbooks and configuration management

solutions, whereas OpsWorks for Puppet Enterprise allows you to configure a Puppet enterprise master Server in AWS. Puppet offers a series of tools to enforce and automate on-demand tasks for your infrastructure.

72. Your company plans to host a web application on a number of EC2 instances and has decided to add a service that would assist in the distribution of traffic through a number of EC2 applications. The main requirements is for the service to scale to one million requests per second. For this requirement, which of the following would you implement?

A. An SQS Queue
B. A Classic Load Balancers
C. A Network Load Balancer
D. An ECS Cluster

Answer: C

Explanation: Using Network Load Balancer rather than Classic Load Balancer has many benefits:

- It can scale millions of requests
- It has the ability to handle dynamic workloads
- It supports static IP address, and you can also enable Elastic IP address per subnet
- It supports to register targets by IP address

73. You have multiple instances in AWS and you want to save the cost by shutting down those instances that are not in use. How can you do this?

A. By checkig the CloudWatch metrics on the underlying EBS volumes. If there is no activity, then you should trigger an alarm to shut down the instance
B. By checking the AWS Config service to check for any configuration changes on the instance. If there are no changes, then trigger an alert to shut down the instance
C. By checking the CloudTrail logs to see if there is any activity on the instance. If not, then trigger an alert to shut down the instance
D. By creating CloudWatch alarms based on a certain metric and then shutting down the instance based on the alarm

Answer: D

Explanation: You can create alarms that stop, terminate, reboot or reboot automated using Amazon CloudWatch alarm actions. You can use stop-or terminate actions to save money if an

instance is no longer necessary. You can reboot and retrieve actions to reboot those instances automatically or reboot them in new hardware where system deficiency occurs.

74. A company is using DynamoDB in its application as backend, which is hosted in AWS. The read and write operation for the database is defined, but in peak loads, the request begins throttling. What can you use from the following to manage huge workloads in peak time?
   A. Place an SQS queue in front of the DynamoDB table
   B. Enable AutoScaling for the DynamoDB table
   C. Add the DynamoDB table to an AutoScaling Group
   D. Place an ELB in front of the DynamoDB table

Answer: B

Explanation: To automatically provisioned the capacity for dynamic workloads on the basis of traffic, you can use DynamoDB AutoScaling. By this, the table and global secondary indexes increase the provision of read and write capacity to handle the sudden traffic increase without throttling the request.

75. A finance sector is using S3 bucket to store sensitive data, and needs to be notified whenever any modification is performed on that data. How can this be done? (Choose 2)
   A. By creating an SQS queue
   B. By enabling S3 server access logging
   C. By setting up an S3 event notification
   D. By creating an SNS topic

Answer: C and D

Explanation: You can set up an S3 event notification on the basis of multiple events like object creation, object deletion, restored object. Then to notify via using SNS topic, create SNS topic which sends and deliver a message on any event occurrence.

76. AWS RDS-MySQL Instance has been created. Manual snapshots of the database are taken occasionally for disaster retrieval scenarios. You need to ensure that no downtime is provided when a snapshot of the database is created. How can you do that?
   A. By ensuring that Multi-AZ is enabled for the database

B. By ensuring that the underlying volume type for the database is SSD

C. By ensuring that the underlying volume type for the database is IOPS

D. By ensuring that the snapshot is only taken during the maintenance window

Answer: C

Explanation: Amazon RDS provides a snapshot storage volume of database that backups the entire DB instance rather than a single database. The creation of snap-shot on a single AZ DB instance results in a brief I/O suspension depending on the size and class of your DB instance, which can last from a couple of seconds to a few minutes. This I/O suspension does not affect multi-AZ DB instances, as backups are taken on standby.

77. An enterprise launched instances in a customized VPC. For instances and subnets, the enterprise has set Security Groups and Network ACL, respectively. The traffic required to reach the instance is not getting there. You are required to diagnose the problem and see why the traffic is not reaching the appropriate destination. In such a situation, what should be used?

A. AWS VPC Flow Logs

B. AWS Trusted Advisor

C. AWS CloudWatch Logs

D. AWS CloudTrail Logs

Answer: A

Explanation: VPC Flow Logs allows you to collect IP traffic information on your VPC to and from the network interfaces. Amazon CloudWatch Logs and Amazon S3 are then used to publish flow log information. You can recover and display the information in the selected location after creating a flow log.

Flow logs can help you with a number of tasks. For instance, to find out why specific traffic does not reach an instance, which in turn helps you to diagnose too restrictive rules for a security group. Flow logs can also be used as a security device to monitor the traffic that is reaching your instance.

78. You have set up an EC2 Instance in a VPC (CIDR 10.0.0.0/16) to host a web based application. You must change the security rules so that the applications are accessible to worldwide users. Also, SSH from a workstation, which has an IP of 20.90.6.7 is needed for the instance. Which of the following Security rules would you add to this application? (Choose 2)

A. Inbound Security Rule of port(22) and Source IP as 20.90.6.7/32
B. Inbound Security Rule of port(22) and Source IP as 0.0.0.0/0
C. Inbound Security Rule of port(80) and Source IP as 10.0.0.0/16
D. Inbound Security Rule of port(80) and Source IP as 0.0.0.0/0

Answer: A and D

Explanation: As you want to ensure that users from all over the world have access to the web application, the source IP range needs to be 0.0.0.0/0, not 10.0.0.0/16 and for SSH connectivity to the instance from the IP needs to be 20.90.6.7/32.

79. The ElastiCache service has been used by your development team for whom a Memcached cluster has been set up. There are alerts of heavy utilization for the cluster after being continuously used. What can be done to fix the problem of heavy CPU usage? (Choose 2)
A. Adding an Elastic Load balancer in front of the cache cluster
B. Using a larger cache node type
C. Adding AutoScaling to the nodes
D. Adding more cache nodes

Answer: B and D

Explanation: CPU utilization metric can be as large as 90% if it is multi-threading. If you exceed that threshold, use a larger cache node type to scale the cache cluster or to add more cache nodes.

80. An enterprise presently manages its data warehouse using the Redshift Cluster. All the information transmitted into the Redshift cluster is now required to be transferred by VPC. How would you fulfill this necessity as the Systems Administrator?
A. By ensuring that the settings are defined in the parameter group
B. By ensuring that the underlying EBS volumes for the cluster are created in the VPC
C. By enabling Amazon Redshift Enhanced VPC Routing
D. By changing the Security Groups for the Cluster to only allow traffic into the VPC'

Answer: C

Explanation: Using Enhanced VPC Routing from Amazon Redshift, you can use the VPC standard functions, such as the VPC Security Groups, network access control lists, VPC endpoints, VPC endpoint policies, the internet gateway, and Domain Name System (DNS) servers. Amazon

Redshift forces all UNLOAD and COPY transmission between your cluster and data repositories through your Amazon VPC. These characteristics are used to handle information flow closely between your Amazon Redshift cluster and other resources. You can also use VPC Flow Logs to control COPY and UNLOAD traffic by using Enhanced VPC routing for route traffic via your VPC.

81. In a private subnet of VPC, you launched an instance, but you observe after launching that its status check has failed. How would you resolve this issue?

A. By rebooting the instance
B. By changing the NACLs to allow the underlying hardware to make the necessary instance status checks
C. By making sure that the instance is launched in a public subnet instead of a private subnet
D. By changing the Security Groups to allow the underlying hardware to make the necessary instance status checks

Answer: A

Explanation: Instance Status Checks track your individual instance's software and network setup. These checks identify issues that need to be repaired by you. If an instance status check fails, the issue can typically be resolved by you (e.g. by rebooting the instance or by making changes to your operating scheme).

82. Your company plans to host AWS services and also wants to buy a support plan. The following are the most important conditions:

• Business hour access to Cloud Support Associates
• 24*7 access to customer support

From the following options, which one is cost effective?

A. Basic
B. Business
C. Developer
D. Enterprise

Answer: C

Explanation: As per given requirement the most minimum costing support plan is the Developer Support Plan.

83. An enterprise is using a number of resources in AWS. An external audit of AWS resources will be carried out. As part of the audit, the recorded API activities linked to the current AWS resources are needed. Which service would meet this requirement?
   A. AWS CloudTrail
   B. AWS Config
   C. AWS Trusted Advisor
   D. AWS CloudWatch Logs

Answer: A

Explanation: AWS CloudTrail is an AWS service that enables you to manage, comply, and operate your AWS account with risk audits. A user, role or AWS service, actions are registered in CloudTrail as events. Actions in the AWS Management Console, AWS Command Line Interface, and AWS SDKs and APIs are part of the event.

84. A company is using EC2 instance to host its application. The instance is in a private subnet and the company wants to use Kinesis Stream. How would this be done?
   A. By using a VPC Endpoint gateway
   B. By ensuring that an internet gateway is attached to the VPC
   C. By ensuring that an Egress-only Internet gateway is attached to the VPC
   D. By use a VPC Endpoint Interface

Answer: D

Explanation: You can use a VPC endpoint interface to maintain the traffic from leaving the Amazon network between your Amazon VPC and Kinesis data streams. There is no internet gateway, NAT device, VPN connection, or AWS Direct Connect link required for VPC endpoint interfaces. AWS PrivateLink that powers Interface VPC endpoint is an AWS technology, which allows personal communication between AWS services via an elastic network interface with private IPs in your Amazon VPC.

85. An organization has a number of instances inside a VPC, and wants to scan them in order to check security vulnerabilities. The scanning is performed as per industry standard "Center for Internet Security (CIS) Benchmarks". Which one of the following can assist you in fulfilling this necessity?
   A. AWS GuardDuty Service
   B. AWS Inspector Service

C. AWS Trusted Advisor

D. AWS Config Service

Answer: B

Explanation: You can use AWS Inspector Service to perform scanning of instances for vulnerabilities. There are 4 rule packages that are available in AWS Inspector: Security Best Practices, Runtime Behavior Analysis, Center for Internet Security, and Common Vulnerabilities.

86. A company has set a VPN connection between its on-premises network and AWS network. They are using VPC Flow Log service to capture IP traffic. The following log is captured: 10 123456789010 eni-abc123de 172.31.41.189 172.8.51.117 39751 3389 6 20 3279 1218430010 1218430070 REJECT OK. Which of the following shows this statement in the correct way?

   A. Host with IP 172.8.51.117 is trying RDP connection using UDP protocol to host with IP 172.31.41.189

   B. Host with IP 172.31.41.189 is trying RDP connection using TCP protocol to host with IP 172.8.51.117

   C. Host with IP 172.8.51.117 is trying RDP connection using TCP protocol to host with IP 172.31.41.189

   D. Host with IP 172.31.41.189 is trying RDP connection using UDP protocol to host with IP 172.8.51.117

Answer: B

Explanation: In the above issue, source IP 172.31.41.189 is attempting to create an RDP session (destination port 3389) with TCP protocol (protocol number 6) at the destination IP address 172.8.51.117.

87. An enterprise is planning on hosting a static website in S3. The static website will be brought up when users browse to http://abc.com domain. You have to create the bucket in S3. Which one of the following should be the bucket name?

   A. abc.com

   B. http://abc1.com

   C. abc1

   D. s3.abc1.com

Answer: A

Explanation: You can use your own domain, such as example.com, to serve your content instead of using an Amazon S3 website endpoint. Amazon S3 supports the hosting of a website in the root domain, together with Amazon Route 53 such as, if you have an example root.com domain.

88. You have two VPCs, VPC A (10.0.0.0/16) and VPC B (20.0.0.0/16). You create a VPC peering link with a "pcx-1a2b1a2b" ID between the two VPCs. To ensure that traffic can flow across both VPCs, which of the following route entries need to be added to the route tables? (Choose 2)
    A. In VPCA (Destination:10.0.0.0/16 and Target: pcx-1a2b1a2b)
    B. In VPCB (Destination:10.0.0.0/16 and Target: pcx-1a2b1a2b)
    C. In VPCA (Destination:20.0.0.0/16 and Target: pcx-1a2b1a2b)
    D. In VPCA (Destination:20.0.0.0/16 and Target: 10.0.0.0/16)

Answer: B and C

Explanation: In VPC A, route table adds route by putting destination as the CIDR of VPC B and target as VPC peering ID. While in VPC B, put destination as VPC A CIDR value and target the VPC peering ID.

89. A number of Lambda functions have been developed by a company who now wants to place them in reusable templates so that it can be used in subsequent deployments in another AWS environment. What service can be used for this requirement?
    A. AWS CloudFormation
    B. AWS Config
    C. AWS CloudTrail
    D. AWS OpsWorks

Answer: A

Explanation: To specify, implement, and configure serverless applications, you can use AWS CloudFormation. It is a service that helps you model and configure your AWS resources and save your time with the management of these resources. It also helps you give more time to your AWS applications. You can create a template describing all the AWS resources you need (such as Lambda and DynamoDB tables). AWS CloudFormation provides and configures the resources for

you. You do not have to create and configure AWS resources individually and figure out what is important—AWS CloudFormation handles everything.

90. An enterprise launches an EC2 instance that goes into the impaired state, and you want it to return to its original state. How can you automate this procedure whenever an instance goes in the impaired state?

A. By creating an AWS Trusted Advisor rule that triggers an alarm, and based on that alarm, creates an action to recover the instance

B. By creating an AWS config rule that triggers an alarm action to recover the instance

C. By creating a CloudWatch alarm, and based on the alarm, creating an action to recover the instance

D. By checking the CloudTrail logs and adding an alarm action to recover the instance

Answer: C

Explanation: Amazon CloudWatch alarm is created to monitor instances. You can automatically recover the instance if it becomes impaired due to an underlying hardware fault or a problem showing that AWS participation needs for repairing of the instance. You can automatically recover the instance. The instance that is recovered is similar to the original instance, including instance ID, Private IP, Elastic IP address, and all metadata. Once the instance is terminated, you will not be able to recover it.

91. A company is using on-premises storage, but now needs to extend the storage on AWS. For storage, the company plans to use S3, and NFS to make files shareable to an on-premises server. What should be used for these requirements?

A. AWS EBS Volumes

B. File Gateway

C. EFS File System

D. S3 Lifecycle Policies

Answer: B

Explanation: File Gateway – A file gateway supports an Amazon Simple Storage Service (Amazon S3) file interface, and combines that service with a virtual software device. This combination enables you to store and retrieve objects in Amazon S3 using standard industrial file protocols such as the Network File System (NFS) and Server Message Block (SMB). The software device or

gateway is used as a Virtual Machine (VM) on your on-site environment, which is operated by VMware ESXi or Microsoft Hyper-V. The gateway offers access to S3 objects as mounting points for file sharing or files.

92. An organization has recently begun to use the Storage Gateway to increase storage ability for AWS Cloud. There is a requirement for the AWS Storage Gateway to encrypt all information at rest. To comply with this request, which of the following would you do?
   A. Use your own master keys to encrypt the data
   B. Use an SSL certificate to encrypt the data
   C. Create an X.509 certificate that can be used to encrypt the data
   D. Use AWS KMS service to support encryption of the data

Answer: D

Explanation: In order to support encryption, AWS Storage Gateway utilizes AWS Key Management Services (AWS KMS). A storage gateway is integrated with AWS KMS to protect the data received, stored, or administered by Storage Gateway using the Customer Master Keys (CMKs) in your account. Similarly, AWS Storage Gateway API can also be used for this. If AWS KMS is not used, the default Amazon S3-Managed Encryption Keys (SSE-S3) will encrypt all AWS information stored by the Storage Gateway service.

93. An organization has a set of EC2 instances for which they want the usage cost report. The company also wants the future prediction of cost and usage. How would this be done?
   A. By using the Cost Explorer
   B. By using the EC2 Explorer
   C. By using the AWS Config tool
   D. By using the AWS Trusted Advisor

Answer: A

Explanation: AWS offers a free cost explorer reporting tool that allows you to evaluate the price, usage of EC2 instance and of Reserved instances. Up to the last 13 months, you can view the information and predict how much you will spend the next three months.

94. A group of instances in a subnet of a VPC is hosted on which a web based application is running. The same type of request from the 52.67.89.10 IP address is coming, and you want to block this traffic. How will you do that?

    A. By creating an Outbound Rule for the NACL that will deny traffic coming from 52.67.89.10/32
    B. By creating an Inbound Rule for the NACL that will deny traffic coming from 52.67.89.10/32
    C. By creating an Outbound rule for the Security Group for the EC2 Instances to ensure that no traffic goes to that IP
    D. By creating an Inbound Rule for the NACL that will deny traffic coming from 52.67.89.10/0

Answer: B

Explanation: As the request is an inbound request, you need to add a rule to NACL for blocking the traffic from the specific IP address.

95. A company has its application hosted on EC2 instance and works with DynamoDB table. The company wants appropriate permission for accessing the table. How will this be done?

    A. By creating Access keys with the required permissions and ensuring that the Access keys are embedded in the application
    B. By creating an IAM group with the required permissions and ensuring the application runs on behalf of the group on the EC2 instance
    C. By creating an IAM user with the required permissions and ensuring the application runs on behalf of the user on the EC2 instance
    D. By create an IAM Role with the required permissions and ensuring that the role is assigned to the EC2 Instance

Answer: D

Explanation: Create an IAM role rather than an IAM user. You can attach this role to EC2 instance on which application is running. This role has permissions that are specified in the policies of the role.

96. You are using AWS organization for managing your company's multiple accounts. Now you want to inform your security team about the security related alarms from all accounts. How can this be done in minimal overhead?

A. By enabling AWS Personal Health Dashboard for multi account view & using IAM identities to grant Security Team members the access to view this

B. By using AWS Personal Health Dashboard & creating CloudWatch Rules at OU level to notify Security Team when a critical security alarm is generated

C. By using AWS Personal Health Dashboard and CloudWatch Rules & notifying the Security Team when a critical security alarm is generated

D. By using AWS Personal Health Dashboard for all accounts, and this will automatically display all alarms in the AWS Management Console

Answer: C

Explanation: To get notified about any activity or issue regarding AWS services, you can configure AWS CloudWatch Events. In the above scenario, a CloudWatch rule could be set for critical security alarms, and the main Security Team members can be notified via an SNS topic. A CloudFormation template is used for automating this entire notification process for all accounts in an AWS Organization.

97. The volume from a snapshot was just recovered and attached to an instance. An application hosting on the instance will use the new EBS volume. When the application was first launched, you noticed some I/O latency. How do you ensure that volumes created from this snapshot are not confronted by the same problem?

A. By ensuring that all blocks on the volume are accessed at least once

B. By ensuring that the volume is created in the same availability zone as the snapshot

C. By ensuring that the volume being created is of the volume type General Purpose SSD

D. By ensuring that the volume being created is of the volume type Provisioned IOPS

Answer: A

Explanation: The peak efficiency of new EBS volumes is achieved when accessible, and no initializations are required (formerly called pre-heating). However, you must initialize (pulling down from Amazon S3 and writing to volume) storage block on volumes restored from snapshots before accessing the Block. This action requires time and can cause the latency of an I/O procedure to increase significantly once each block is accessed. After the information is accessed once, performance is restored.

You can avoid this performance hit in a production environment by reading from all of the blocks on your volume before you use it; this process is called initialization. For a new volume created from a snapshot, you should read all the blocks that have data before using the volume.

98. An enterprise is using Hadoop cluster that is running on its on-premises, and now needs to shift it to AWS. How could this be done for the transition of workload?

A. AWS RDS
B. AWS Redshift
C. AWS DynamoDB
D. AWS EMR

Answer: D

Explanation: Amazon EMR is a cluster platform that makes running large-scale data frameworks easier for AWS to process and evaluate a huge amount of data. The frameworks are Hadoop or Apache Spark. You can process data for analytical purposes and business intelligent workload by using the frames and associated open source programs, such as Apache Hive and Apache Pig. Furthermore, you can use Amazon EMR for processing and shifting big amount of data in and out of other AWS databases and storage systems, such as Amazon Simple Storage Service (Amazon S3) and Amazon DynamoDB.

99. An organization has its AWS account on which it is hosting multiple contents on S3. The organization wants that a specific S3 bucket's content is available for a limited amount of time. How can this be done?

A. By granting access keys based on a time interval
B. By specifying a time limit in the Bucket ACL
C. By creating an IAM Role with a session duration parameter
D. By creaing an IAM user with a session duration parameter

Answer: C

Explanation: You can specify a value for the parameter DurationSeconds by using an AWS CLI or API operation to assume a role. The length of the role session can be specified by using this parameter from 900 seconds (15 minutes) to a maximum CLI / API session. You should view this setting for your role before you define the parameter. If you specify a value that is greater than the maximum setting for the DurationSeconds parameter, the operation will fail.

100. You have a private subnet in VPC on which a set of instances is placed. The instances need to download the patches from the internet with minimal maintenance for the device

management to relay traffic. Also, they require minimal bandwidth restriction. What can you use for this?

A. Internet Gateway
B. NAT Gateway
C. VPN Connection
D. NAT Instance

Answer: B

Explanation: With the use of NAT gateway, you do not need to perform any maintenance. everything is managed by AWS. It is also capable of scaling bandwidth up to 45 Gbps.

101. You are using EBS volumes for storing critical documents, and you want DR procedure by automating the process of updating of snapshots. How would you do this?

A. AWS Config
B. AWS CloudTrail
C. AWS API Gateway
D. AWS Lambda

Answer: D

Explanation: Amazon EBS issues notifications for various snapshot and encryption status modifications depending on Amazon CloudWatch events. You can set the rules for programmatic actions in CloudWatch Events in response to a snapshot change or encryption. For instance, you can trigger an AWS Lambda to share the completed snapshot with another account or copy it to another disaster recovery region when a snapshot is created.

102.   A company plans to use AWS to roll out its manufacturing. Automation for deployment is intended to be implemented in order to generate a LAMP stack automatically, to download a PHP from S3 and to set up the ELB. Which of the AWS services listed above complies with the necessity to implement the software orderly?

A. AWS OpsWorks
B. AWS CloudFront
C. AWS Elastic Beanstalk
D. AWS CloudFormation

Answer: C

Explanation: We can upload the code, and Elastic Beanstalk handles the deployment automatically from the provisioning capacity, load balance, self-scaling and application health tracking. In the meantime, the AWS resources used in the application are kept in control and the underlying resources can be accessed at any time. It is an easy to use service for deploying and scaling web applications.

103. Your team now has an AWS AutoScaling group to handle EC2 instances for an implementation dynamically. There are currently some problems in the implementation, and the team has to debug what the issue is. How can this be achieved?

    A. By suspending the scaling process so that you can carry out the investigation on the underlying instances

    B. By using the AWS Config to take a configuration snapshot of the Instances and then carrying out the investigation on the underlying Instances

    C. By deleting the Launch Configuration so that you can carry out the investigation on the underlying instances

    D. By deleting the AutoScaling Group so that you can carry out the investigation on the underlying instances

Answer: A

Explanation: You can suspend and resume one or more of your Auto Scaling group's scaling procedures. This can be helpful if you want to explore your web application's settings problem or other problems, then change your application without invoking scaling. AutoScaling can suspend AutoScaling Group processes that fail to launch instances repeatedly. This is called an administrative suspension and is most commonly applicable to AutoScaling groups that try to launch instances for more than 24 hours but have failed to start instances at all. For administrative reasons, you can resume processes that are suspended.

104. An enterprise has an application whose MySQL database is hosted on RDS and webserver on EC2 instance. After ten days, one of the key application tables was accidentally dropped and instantly recovered. Which Amazon RDS function lets you restore your database reliably within 5 minutes of deletion?

    A. RDS Read Replicas

    B. Multi-AZ RDS

    C. RDS Automated Backup

D. RDS Snapshots

Answer: C

Explanation: Amazon RDS generates automatic DB instance backups and saves them. Amazon RDS provides a snapshot of your DB instance for the storage volume and not just for single databases, supporting the entire DB instance. In the backup window of your DB instance, Amazon RDS generates automatic backups of your DB instance. Amazon RDS saves your DB instance's automated backups based on the retention period you specify. If required, during the backup retention period, you can retrieve your database anytime.

105.   You deploy several templates for CloudFormation. You get some errors when deploying the templates such as Throttling, Sender and Rate exceed. How would you resolve these issues?

A. By adding an exponential backoff between the calls to the createStack API
B. By combining the stacks into one template and deploying the stack
C. By adding a pause in the CloudFormation templates
D. By using a large instance from where the CloudFormation template is being deployed

Answer: A

Explanation: Because of too many resource are being created at the same time using Stack API, this error occurs. To overcome this issue, you can use the exponential backoff concept to insert delays in requests.

106.   A financial institute is using a huge amount of EC2 instances and now wants to ensure that no critical security flaw occurs on any of the servers. What can be used for this? (Choose 2)

A. AWS SSM to patch the servers
B. AWS Inspector to patch the servers
C. AWS Inspector to ensure that the servers have no critical flaws
D. AWS Config to ensure that the servers have no critical flaws

Answer: A and C

Explanation: Amazon Inspector is an automated security evaluation service to enhance the security and compliance of AWS apps. Amazon Inspector automatically evaluates vulnerability and deviations from best practices for apps. Amazon Inspector generates a comprehensive list of security finding, prioritized by severity after conducting the evaluation. These results are

accessible via a console or API of the Amazon Inspector directly or as part of comprehensive evaluation reports.

107. You manage your business presently with an AWS RDS instance. Whenever the AWS RDS database backup happens, you need to be notified. How can you do that as easily as possible? (Choose 2)
   A. By creating an SNS topic
   B. By subscribing to AWS RDS Events service
   C. By adding a Lambda trigger to the AWS RDS database
   D. By creating an SQS queue for the event messages

Answer: A and B

Explanation: Amazon RDS categorizes these events so that you can subscribe to them when needed. If an incident in the category takes place, you will be notified. A DB instance, DB security group, DB cluster, DB snapshot, DB cluster snapshot, or a DB parameter group can also be subscribed to this category. For example, if you subscribe for a certain DB instance in the Backup class, you are notified of a backup event that affects the DB instance whenever there is a backup event. You are informed when a DB security group is altered if you subscribe with a Configuration Change category for a DB security group. When an event notification subscription changes, you also obtain a notification.

108. An organization wants to use EC2 instances for batch processing application. For application hosting, it needs to spin up the instances. What type of instance should the organization choose for this requirement?
   A. Storage Optimized
   B. Memory Optimized
   C. General Optimized
   D. Compute Optimized

Answer: D

Explanation: The compute optimized instances are perfect for high-performance compute-bound apps. The following apps are well adapted:

- Batch processing workloads
- Media transcoding
- High-performance web servers

- High-performance computing (HPC)
- Scientific modeling
- Dedicated gaming servers and ad serving engines
- Machine learning inference and other compute-intensive applications

109. An online marketing company has its website, whose related images are stored in S3. The company is using CloudFront distribution with S3 as an origin, for better user experience. During monitoring, it was observed that some users reach the bucket directly without using CloudFront distribution and downloading images. How can you overcome this issue? (Choose 2)

A. By ensuring that only the IAM user has access to read objects from the S3 bucket
B. By ensuring that only the CloudFront Origin Access Identity has access to read objects from the S3 bucket
C. By creating a separate IAM user
D. By creating a CloudFront Origin Access Identity

Answer: B and D

Explanation: The following tasks are performed, regardless of whether the URLs are signed, to ensure your users access your object using only CloudFront URLs:

- Create an Origin Access Identity, which is a special CloudFront user, and associate the Origin Access Identity with your distribution. You can also create an origin access identity and add it to your distribution when you create the distribution
- Change permissions on either your Amazon S3 bucket or the items on your bucket to allow read only to the Origin Access Identity. The CloudFront Origin Access Identity receives the items for your customers when your customers reach your Amazon S3 items through CloudFront. Origin Access Identity has the right in your Amazon S3 bucket to have access to objects but not for users to directly access the bucket

110. An enterprise has its S3 bucket in the Central region. The items must now be replicated from the bucket to another region based on compliance. In order to replicate, which of the following measures are necessary? (Choose 2)

A. The source and destination buckets must be in same AWS Region
B. The source and destination buckets must have encryption enabled
C. The source and destination buckets must have versioning enabled

D. The source and destination buckets must be in different AWS Regions

Answer: C and D

Explanation: For cross region replication, your source and destination bucket must enable versioning, both buckets must be in a separate region, and S3 must have appropriate permissions to replicate the item from source to destination.

111. You are using DynamoDB tables and need to protect and recover the tables in case of accidental write and deletion. How can you do this?
    A. By using Point-in-time recovery feature
    B. By enabling MultiAZ
    C. By enabling global tables
    D. By enabling AutoScaling

Answer: A

Explanation: You are able to allow point-in-time recovery and generate on-demand backups for your Amazon DynamoDB tables. Point-in-time recovery enables to prevent accidental write or remove activities in your Amazon DynamoDB tables. You do not have to worry about the creation, maintenance or schedule of on-demand backups in Point-in-time recovery. You can restore the table to any point of time in the last 35 days with point-in-time recovery. DynamoDB keeps incremental table backups.

112. A financial institute has two accounts. One is the audited account, and the other is technical account. The staff users of audit account need limited access to the technical account for auditing. How can this be accessed in a securable way?
    A. By creating an IAM user in the production AWS account and sharing the access keys then ensuring the IAM user is part of a secure group
    B. By creating an IAM user in the production AWS account and sharing the password for the console access
    C. By creating a cross account role and sharing the ARN for the role
    D. By creating an IAM user in the production AWS account and sharing the access keys

Answer: C

Explanation: A user in one account can change to the role of the same account or another. During using this role, the user only has access to the actions and resources that the role allows; initial user permissions are suspended. The initial user permissions are restored once the user leaves the position.

113. A company placed its EC2 instance in a private subnet (10.1.1.0/24). The instance wants to download updates from the internet via HTTPS. NAT instance is in the public subnet. What rule does the company need to add in SG as an incoming rule of NAT instance?

    A. Allow Incoming from Source 0.0.0.0/0 on port 443
    B. Allow Incoming from Source 10.1.1.0/24 on port 443
    C. Allow Incoming from Source 0.0.0.0/0 on port 80
    D. Allow Incoming from Source 10.1.1.0/24 on port 80

Answer: B

Explanation: The rule, which they need to add in the SG is the incoming request from the private subnet's instance from port 443, which is for HTTPS.

114. You have a number of instances in one region and you want to make these instances available in another region. How would you do this? (Choose 2)

    A. By making an AMI of the EC2 Instance
    B. By copying the underlying EBS volume to the destination region
    C. By copying the AMI to the destination region
    D. By copying the underlying EC2 Instance to the destination region

Answer: A and C

Explanation: You may use the AWS Management Console, SDKs or the Amazon EC2 API for copying an Amazon Machine Image (AMI) within or another region, which supports the CopyImage action. The copying image is free. So first create an AMI of instance and then copy it in your desired region.

115. A company stores all critical records in the Amazon S3 bucket. A non-compliant matter for non-maintenance of access logs to those buckets was raised during the annual audit. You plan

to allow Amazon S3 Server Access Logs for all of these buckets as a SysOps administrator. Which option suggests to store Amazon S3 Server Access Logs?

A. Source & Target bucket should be the same bucket & should be created in the same AWS region

B. Source & Target bucket should be the same bucket & should be created in different AWS regions

C. Source & Target bucket should be separate bucket & should be created in different AWS regions

D. Source & Target bucket should be separate bucket & should be created in the same AWS region

Answer: D

Explanation: It is recommended for Source bucket & target bucket to be separated to easily manage the logs for storage of the Amazon S3 server access logs. Both should own a single account and be in the same region of AWS.

116. An educational institute wants to create a VPC with a public subnet and private subnet. In private subnet, there is instance whose traffic needs to be routed to the internet via NAT gateway that is placed in the public subnet. What routes need to be added in the main and custom route tables?

A. In the custom route table, add a route with destination of 0.0.0.0/0 and the NAT gateway ID

B. In the main route, table add a route with destination of 0.0.0.0/0 and the Internet gateway ID

C. In the main route, table add a route with destination of 0.0.0.0/0 and the NAT gateway ID

D. In the custom route table add a route with destination of 0.0.0.0/0 and the Internet gateway ID

Answer: C and D

Explanation: A custom route table is linked with a public subnet, so they need to add a rule with destination 0.0.0.0/0 and Internet Gateway ID. These route tables enable the instances in the subnet to communicate with each other in a VPC or to the internet via internet gateway. All communication are done over IPv4.

The main Route table is linked with a private subnet, so you need to add a rule with destination 0.0.0.0/0 and NAT gateway ID. The route tables enable the instances in the subnet to

communicate with each other or with the internet via NAT gateway. All these communications are done over IPv4.

117. You have a VPC (10.0.0.0/16) with public subnet (10.0.2.0/24) and private subnet (10.0.1.0/24). Now you want to host your web server on public subnet and database server on a private subnet with port 80 and 3306, respectively. The database server is safely connected to the web server. A user sets up a NAT instance Security group. Which of the following entries are not needed for the NAT Security Group? (Choose 2)

A. For Outbound, allow Destination: 10.0.1.0/24 on port 80
B. For Outbound, allow Destination: 0.0.0.0/0 on port 443
C. For Inbound, allow Source: 10.0.2.0/24 on port 80
D. For Inbound, allow Source: 10.0.1.0/24 on port 80

Answer: A and C

Explanation: For internet access, NAT instance is used in a secure way for private subnet, which does not have direct internet access. So destination must be the internet, not the private subnet. While the public subnet does not need to use NAT instance to communicate with internet. As this is public subnet with public IP, it has direct access to the internet.

118. A newly developed application is hosted in AWS on which performance testing is being conducted. An issue arrives when the testing team requests the IT team for a new structure and to scale the infrastructure. How can you, as a SysOps administrator, automate this process? (Choose 2)

A. By creating a target group in the load balancer
B. By creating an Elastic Load Balancer
C. By ensuring that the AutoScaling Group creates new instances based on instance utilization
D. By creating an AutoScaling Group and launching configuration

Answer: C and D

Explanation: When configuring dynamic scaling, you must specify how you want to scale depending on requirements as per demands. You have a web application currently running in two cases, for example, and you do not want to exceed 70% of the CPU usage of the Auto-Scaling group. The AutoScaling group can be configured to automatically scale to fulfill this requirement. This sort of policy determines how the scaling is done.

119. An instance in the VPC needs to support high bandwidth and high packet per second performance. What should you do to fulfill this requirement?
    A. Consider using Elastic IP addresses
    B. Use Instance types that support Enhanced Networking
    C. Use EBS Optimized Instance types
    D. Consider using placement groups

Answer: B

Explanation: Single root I/O virtualization (Sr-IOV) is used in enhanced networking to provide the highest possible networking functions on supported instances. SR-IOV is a virtualization device technique that delivers greater I/O performance and less CPU usage than traditional virtualized network interfaces. Higher bandwidth, greater packet per second (PPS) efficiency and continuously reduced inter-instance latencies are provided through enhanced networking. For enhanced networking, there is no extra charge.

120. An organization produces digital policy documents that are needed for verification by the administrators. When documents are checked, the compliance problem may not be needed in the future. As the Sysops Administrator, after verification, you were asked to build an appropriate data store for the records. Which would be the best cost-effective choice?
    A. AWS RDS
    B. AWS S3- Standard Storage
    C. AWS S3- RRS
    D. AWS Glacier

Answer: D

Explanation: Amazon Glacier is an incredibly low-costing storage service that offers lasting storage with information archival and backup characteristics. Customers can save their information efficiently with Amazon Glacier for months, years or decades. Amazon Glacier allows clients to offload the operating and scaling burdens of AWS storage, so the organization does not need to worry about capacity provisioning, information replication, hardware failure detecting and recovering, hardware provisioning or hardware transitions.

121. You want to query data from CSV file that is stored in S3. You do not want to use any code for this nor use any service for this purpose if possible. Which of the following service can you use for this purpose?

A. AWS Redshift
B. AWS DynamoDB
C. AWS Athena
D. AWS Glacier

Answer: C

Explanation: Amazon Athena is an interactive query service for analyzing information directly using standard SQL on Amazon Simple Storage Service (Amazon S3). You can point Athena to your information in Amazon S3 using a number of actions in the AWS Management Console and start using standard SQL to perform ad-hoc queries to get outcomes in seconds.

122. You have established a web server with AutoScaling group that sits behind Application Load Balancer. You need to capture all traffic between client and web server as part of the security requirement. You plan to activate Access logs on Application Load Balancer but are unsure about the traffic that has been captured by allowing this log. What is true about the Access log entries for Application Load Balancer?

A. It does not log traffic when there are no healthy targets remaining to respond to client requests
B. It does not log health check requests from Application Load Balancer to the target group
C. It does not log WSS (web socket over SSL/TLS) traffic between client & target group
D. It does not capture malformed requests from clients to the target server

Answer: B

Explanation: Application Load Balancer Access logs consist of all requests not forwarded to targets, but not any request for health inspections that ALB regularly sends to target groups.

123. Your firm uses S3 to store your company's critical information. Several users currently have full access for S3 buckets within your group. You need to find a way not to affect your users and protect from accidental object deletion. In what way can you do this? (Choose 2)

A. By enabling object life cycle policies and configuring the data older than 3 months to be archived in Glacier

B. By enabling versioning on your S3 Buckets
C. By creating a Bucket policy and allowing read only permissions to all users at the bucket level
D. By configuring your S3 Buckets with MFA delete

Answer: B and D

Explanation: Versioning is a way to maintain several variants of an object in the same bucket. The versioning of any item stored in your Amazon S3 bucket can be used to preserve, recover and restore all versions of it. With versioning, both unintended user actions and application failures are easy to recover. You can also add security by enabling MFA to delete the bucket.

124. An auditing firm is presently conducting an infrastructure audit. They want to understand what kinds of safety processes are introduced in AWS data centers. How would you meet this requirement?
A. By using a document from the AWS Artifact web service
B. By contacting an AWS Direct Connect partner
C. By sending a copy of the AWS Security Whitepapers
D. By raising a call with AWS Support to get a tour of the data center

Answer: A

Explanation: On-demand downloads for AWS security and compliance documents are made available by AWS Artifact including AWS ISO certifications, Payment Card Industry (PCI) and Service Organization Control (SOC) reports. You can submit your auditors or regulators with the security and compliance documents (also known as auditing devices) for the demonstration of your AWS infrastructure and services. You can also use these papers as instructions to assess your own cloud architecture and the effectiveness of the internal controls of your company.

125. You work for a big IT company as a SysOps Administrator. In your enterprise, multiple accounts are developed that enable staff to generate AWS resources according to the project needs. Last week, an Amazon S3 bucket was developed by a staff member with no Object Level Policy, resulting in public access to critical project documents. You plan to block public access settings for all S3 buckets to prevent such problems in the future. When implementing these configurations at various levels, which of the following should be the limitations regarded?

A. Amazon S3 applies a restrictive combination of object level & bucket level setting per AWS region that applies for current buckets

B. Amazon S3 applies a restrictive combination of bucket level & account level setting per AWS region that applies for all current & future buckets

C. Amazon S3 applies a restrictive combination of bucket level & account level setting to all regions globally that applies for all current & future buckets

D. Amazon S3 applies a restrictive combination of object level & bucket level setting to all regions globally that applies only for future buckets

Answer: C

Explanation: To avoid public access, block public access settings can be implemented at buckets or account levels to protect the Amazon S3 bucket. A restrictive mixture of both settings; buckets and account levels are applied to all existing and future buckets produced in this account. Additionally, in all AWS regions, these settings are applied. Users can not create a publicly available S3 bucket by applying these configurations unless explicitly permitted.

126. In the EU region, an enterprise has a Redshift cluster. In case of problems in the main area, the enterprise must guarantee that the cluster is accessible in another area. What can be done to fulfill this requirement?

A. Enable Read Replica's for the Redshift cluster

B. Enable global tables for the Redshift cluster

C. Enable Multi-AZ for the Redshift cluster

D. Copy a snapshot of the cluster to another region

Answer: D

Explanation: You can set Amazon Redshift to copy snapshots for a cluster automatically into another region. When a snapshot is created in the primary region (source region) of the cluster, it is copied into a secondary region which is called the destination region. You will be able to restore the cluster of your recent data if something affects the primary region by storing a copy of your snapshots in another region.

127. You plan to set up an AWS application. This application hosts a general purpose workload app. You want to create a cost effective instance that can also be flexible for application spikes. To which of the following can be implemented for this requirement? (Choose 2)

A. Configure the t2 unlimited option

B. Configure a t2.micro instance

C. Configure a c4.large instance

D. Configure burstable performance on the instance

Answer: A and B

Explanation: T2 Unlimited is a setup option for T2 instances that are set for a running or stopped T2 instance at the launch or at any time. T2 Unlimited instances can burst above the baseline for as long as required. This enables you to enjoy the low T2 instance hourly price for a wide variety of general-purpose applications and ensures that your instances are never held to the baseline performance. All CPU usage peaks are automatically included in the basic T2 hourly instance price where average T2 unlimited instance if CPU utilization is at or below the baseline during a rolling 24-hour period.

128. An enterprise has its webserver hosted in on-premises. Now, it wants to check the health of the system. In case the health degrades for any reason, it should switch to static website hosted on AWS. How would the company do this?

    A. By using AWS Opsworks to check for issues in the on-premises webserver and then failing over to an environment defined in AWS Opsworks

    B. By using Elastic Beanstalk to check for issues in the on-premises webserver and then failing over to an environment defined in Elastic Beanstalk

    C. By using an Elastic Load balancer to divert traffic when the on-premises webserver has issues

    D. By using Route 53 health checks to failover to the secondary site if the on-premises webserver has issues

Answer: D

Explanation: Use active-passive failover setting when you want a primary resource or a resource group to be made available most of the time, and if all primary resources are unavailable, you should have a secondary resource or resource group on standby. Route 53 only involves healthy primary resources when responding to queries. In the case of unhealthy primary resources, Route 53 starts to include only the healthy secondary resources as a response to DNS queries.

129. A financial institute is using DynamoDB tables for storing the data. Now it wants to be able to know about the amount of read and write capacity that is utilized. How would this be done?

    A. By using AWS Config logs to see the amount of Read and Write Capacity being utilized

    B. By using CloudTrail logs to see the amount of Read and Write Capacity being utilized

    C. By using CloudWatch metrics to see the amount of Read and Write Capacity being utilized

D. By using CloudWatch logs to see the amount of Read and Write Capacity being utilized

Answer: C

Explanation: With Amazon CloudWatch service, you can monitor the DynamoDB tables. During the given period, you can check ConsumedReadCapacityUnits or ConsumedWriteCapacityUnits to monitor the amount of your provisioned throughput being used.

130.   An organization wants to use AWS service for its 3-tier application's data store with the following requirements:
   - Multi schema changing ability
   - Database should be relational and durable
   - Any modification in a database should not give downtime

   What service can they use for this purpose?
   A. AWS Aurora
   B. AWS S3
   C. AWS Redshift
   D. AWS DynamoDB

Answer: A

Explanation: In Amazon Aurora, you can almost instantly run a DDL (Data Definition Language) quickly for an ALTER TABLE procedure. It finishes operations with no need to copy the table and without material effect in other DML statements. As there is no time consumption of table copy storage, even for big tables on small instances, it makes DDL statements practical. Amazon Aurora is a MySQL compatible database that combines high-end business databases, availability and speed with the ease and cost effectiveness of open-source databases.

131. Your merchant wants to access your AWS resource from your account, so you create an AWS user. Now you want to restrict the access of that user to the specific resource via policy. What is an ideal policy that you can use?
   A. A bucket ACL
   B. An Inline Policy
   C. An AWS Managed Policy
   D. A Bucket Policy

Answer: B

Explanation: Inline policies are useful if a strict one-to-one relationship between a policy and the principal entity it applies to, is to be maintained. For example, you want to make sure that the permissions in policy are not assigned inadvertently to a principal entity other than the one for which they are intended.

If you use an inline policy, you cannot associate the permissions in the policy to the false entity, even accidentally. Moreover, the policies incorporated into the principal entity are also removed when you use the AWS Management Console. This is because they belong to the principal entity.

132.   Recently, your business implemented AWS webservers. Web developers in your company need to use corporate AD credentials to access these servers. For this, you developed a SAML identity provider in AWS IAM console. Which AWS-specific attributes of the ID Provider, apart from NameID, are needed? (Choose 3)

    A. Audience
    B. ProviderID
    C. Role
    D. RoleSessionName
    E. SessionID

Answer: A, C and D

Explanation: The attributes that are required to be present in SAML Assertion are: roles, audience & RolesSessionName, along with nameID. these need to be sent to AWS STS in order to fulfill the requirement.

133. You established an AutoScaling Group and need to know when it scales and adds new instances. Which services can achieve this if used in conjunction with AutoScaling Group?

    A. AWS ELB
    B. AWS SQS
    C. AWS SNS
    D. AWS SWF

Answer: C

Explanation: If you are using Amazon EC2 AutoScaling, then it is helpful to know when Amazon EC2 Auto Scaling starts or terminates EC2 instances in your AutoScaling group to scale your

application automatically. Amazon SNS coordinates and manages the delivery or sending of a notification to subscribed customers or endpoints. If you are using your AutoScaling Group scales, you can configure Amazon EC2 to send an SNS notification.

134.   You are using dual VPN connection between your on-premises and AWS of which you want a redundant link. From the following, which will be helpful for this situation?
    A. Since it is a dual VPN connection, there is already redundancy in place
    B. Create a secondary VPN connection
    C. Create an internet gateway connection
    D. Create a NAT gateway connection

Answer: B

Explanation: Two tunnels are provided to guarantee a site-to-site VPN link in the event of unavailability of one of the VPN links. You may establish a second site-to-site VPN link to your VPC and virtual personal gateway using a second customer gateway to ensure protection against loss of connectivity when your customer gateway is inaccessible. You can perform maintenance on one of your customer gateways using redundant site-to-site VPN links and customer gateways, while traffic flows across a Site-to-Site VPN secondary customer gateway. You need to create a second VPN site-to-site link to create redundant site-to-site VPN links and customer gateway on your remote network. The second VPN site-to-site connection's client gateway IP address must be available openly (publicly).

135.   A company has its data warehousing in its on-site location and now need to shift to AWS. Which service can you use to migrate the data in the easiest way possible?
    A. AWS Database Migration Service
    B. AWS S3 Lifecycle Policy
    C. AWS CloudWatch
    D. AWS CloudTrail

Answer: A

Explanation: AWS Database Migration Service (AWS DMS) is a cloud service that facilitates the transfer of relational databases, data warehouse, NoSQL databases and other data storage types. AWS DMS can be used to migrate your data to AWS Cloud, to on-site instances or to settings between combinations of cloud and on-site.

136. An educational institute uses S3 bucket to store its student's critical information. Now the senior staff members need a Get, Put and Delete access to all folders individually. This policy is also needed to be implemented in future to other staff members. What is the right "Resource parameter" in policy declaration that can be implemented to fulfill this requirement?

```
{
   "Version":"2012-10-17",
   "Statement":[
     {
        "Effect":"Allow",
        "Action":[
           "s3:PutObject",
           "s3:GetObject",
           "s3:DeleteObject",
        ],
        "Resource":"_____"
     }
   ]
}
```

A. "Resource":"arn:aws:s3:::<bucketname>/${aws:userid}/*"
B. "Resource":"arn:aws:s3:::<bucketname>/${aws:username}/*"
C. "Resource":"arn:aws:s3:::<bucketname>/*"
D. "Resource":"arn:aws:s3:::<bucketname>/UserA/*" (create for each individual user)

Answer: A

Explanation: An individual policy can be set with a policy variable and linked to a group instead of generating multiple access policies for every user. So add all user in a single group. Using${ aws: userid} policy variable, an access policy is created that assesses the user ID for each user and grants access only to the folders based on this user ID by defining actions.

137. If you have AWS users, then how can you manage the security credentials in AWS by using best practices? (Choose 3)

A. By granting access on a least privilege basis

B. By using the AWS Root access keys for critical applications to access AWS resources
C. By enabling MFA for Privileged users
D. By using IAM Roles for EC2 Instances

Answer: A, B and D

Explanation: In order to secure your AWS resource, the best practices of IAM are:

- Grant Least Privilege
- Enable MFA
- Use Roles for applications that run on Amazon EC2 Instances
- Use Roles to delegate permissions
- Rotate credentials regularly
- Use Policy Conditions for extra security

138. A fresh intranet site is being designed by the developer team that will access a bucket to get information material. You have been told by the Security Team to create rigorous access policies for S3 bucket with least privileges. What can be used for the implementation of the policy, including ensuring minimum operational adjustments after original deployment?

A. Allow "s3:GetObject" to access S3 bucket with a "StringLike" condition matching URL & deny all other actions on this S3 bucket from an intranet web-site

B. Allow "s3:GetObject" action on S3 bucket with a condition using "IPAddress" matching IP range in "aws:SourceIp" key & deny all other actions on this S3 bucket using the condition "NotIpAddress"

C. Allow "s3:GetObject" action on S3 bucket with a condition using "IPAddress" matching specific IP in "aws:SourceIp" key & deny all other actions on this S3 bucket using the condition "NotIpAddress"

D. Allow "s3:GetObject" to access S3 bucket with a "StringLike" condition using "aws:Referer" key & deny all other actions on this S3 bucket from an intranet web-site

Answer: D

Explanation: Using "aws:Referer" key, a Get request is originated from the specific web-site for allowing access to S3 bucket. In the above scenario, an "s3:GetObject" can be created matching "StringLike" condition & key as "aws:Referer" to match specific web-site pages that would only have access to read objects from S3 buckets.

139.   An enterprise plans to use AWS RDS for its database and needs to forecast the expenses. On what factors does the cost element depend? (Choose 3)
A. The number of hours the database is running
B. The instance type for the database server
C. The storage allocated to the server
D. The amount of data transferred to an EC2 Instance in the same region

Answer: A, B and C

Explanation: The billing of RDS instance is based on DB instance hours, storage, I/O requests, backup storage, data transfer and type of instance.

140.   An organization has VPC and in the private subnet of VPC, servers are placed that need to communicate to the external networks. How would the organization meet this requirement?
A. By adding a bastion host in a public subnet
B. By adding a bastion host in a private subnet
C. By changing the Route tables for the subnet to add the internet gateway
D. By changing the Route tables for the subnet to add the NAT gateway

Answer: A

Explanation: In the Amazon Web Service (AWS), a bastion host is defined as a "server to provide access to a private network from an external network such as the internet. A bastion host must minimize the chances of penetration due to exposure to potential attacks.

141.There are a number of EBS volumes in your company and you are required to make sure that the EBS volumes are automatically backed up. What would you use for this purpose?
A. AWS Config
B. AWS Inspector
C. AWS Data Lifecycle Manager
D. S3 Lifecycle Policies

Answer: C

Explanation: With AWS Data Lifecycle Manager, you can automatically create, retain and delete the snapshots of EBS volumes that is used for backup. Automating the management of snapshots will help you:

•   Reduce the cost of storage by removing old backups

- For auditors and complains, retain the backups
- Protect data by scheduling the regular backups

142. A company host its application on AWS for which it is planning a DR procedure. The company wants that when the primary site goes down, the duration of downtime is as less as possible. What is the ideal solution for this?
   A. Pilot Light
   B. Backup and restore
   C. Warm standby
   D. Multi-site

Answer: D

Explanation: With Multi-site DR strategy, you have the least downtime as per DR spectrum.

143. A banking sector uses EC2 instances for its application and wants to log files for future processes of EC2 instance in S3 bucket. How would this be done?
   A. AWS Redshift
   B. AWS DataPipeline
   C. AWS DynamoDB
   D. AWS Athena

Answer: B

Explanation: AWS Data Pipeline is a web-based service that you can use to automate information conversion and motion. You can set data-driven workflows with the AWS Data Pipeline so that tasks can depend on effective execution of the prior task. You identify the data transformation parameters and AWS Data Pipeline complies with the logic that you have set up.

144. What does the policy given below perform?

```
{
    "Version": "2012-10-17",
    "Id": "123",
```

```
"Statement": [
  {
    "Sid": "",
    "Effect": "Deny",
    "Principal": "*",
    "Action": "s3:*",
    "Resource": "arn:aws:s3:::examplebucket/taxdocuments/*",
    "Condition": { "Null": { "aws:MultiFactorAuthAge": true }}
  }
 ]
}
```

A. Denies access to the Bucket if the user is not authenticating via MFA device
B. Denies access to the bucket if the user has used an MFA device for authentication
C. Allows access to the bucket if the IAM user has successfully logged into the console using Access keys
D. Allows access to the bucket if the IAM user has successfully logged into the console using a password

Answer: A

Explanation: The aws: MultiFactorAuthAge key gives a numerical value showing how long a temporary credential has been generated (in seconds) when Amazon S3 gets an MFA authentication application. If no MFA system has produced the temporary credential supplied to the application, the key value is null. A condition illustrated in the question verifies this value under a bucket policy. This policy rejects any operation of Amazon S3 on the /taxdocuments folder in the bucket if the application is not authenticated by MFA. Null condition in the condition block is valid if the key value of aws: MultiFactorAuthAge is null, meaning temporary security credentials were created without the MFA key.

145. You now have an AWS account for your company. An audit approaches and the required artifacts must be ready to assist the audit. What should you be accountable for in the audit according to the AWS Responsibility model? (Choose 2)
A. The access keys rotation policy for your IAM users
B. Physical security for the AWS Data Centers
C. The underlying Security Groups for your EC2 Instances
D. The global infrastructure that hosts the virtualization hypervisors

Answer: A and C

Explanation: Global infrastructure and physical security are the responsibilities of AWS. Customers responsibility is to look after their data, platform, OS, IAM and application. They are also responsible for client side encryption, server side encryption, firewall and network configurations, and network traffic protection.

146. If your application running on an EC2 instance is facing a problem, and you want to resolve this issue by upgrading the instance type. How will you do this?
    A. By detaching the underlying ENI and then changing the Instance Type
    B. By detaching the underlying EBS volumes and then changing the Instance Type
    C. By directly changing the instance type from the AWS Console
    D. By stopping the instance and then changing the Instance Type

Answer: D

Explanation: To change the instance type, you must stop the instance. After changing the instance type when you start, it must be aware of the following things:

- Instance ID does not change, but it can be moved to new hardware
- Previous Public IP is hanged with a new one
- If it is in ASG, it is considered as unhealthy. It is terminated and a replacement instance is launched
- Make sure you are planning to stop your instance. It could take a few minutes to stop and resize an instance. Restarting your instance can also take time based on the start-up scripts of your application

147. A load balancer has been set up in AWS. You have configured EC2 Instances in multiple AZs and made sure the load balancer also has these AZs. How will the traffic in each of the Availability Zones be spread across the registered targets?
    A. By enabling connection draining
    B. By enabling cross-zone load balancing
    C. By enabling Sticky Sessions
    D. By enabling proxy protocol

Answer: B

Explanation: The load balancer nodes distribute customer requests to registered targets. Each load balancer node distributes traffic across the registered targets in all Availability Zones, if the cross-zone load balancing is activated. Each Load Balancer node distributes traffic through its Availability Zone only when cross-zone load balance is disabled.

148. A set of customer master keys is described in AWS KMS. You, as the SysOps Administrator need to check who has access to the keys and also want to make the necessary adjustments on the basis of your company's policy. What can you modify to know who has access to the keys in KMS service?
    A. Key Policies
    B. Object ACLs
    C. Bucket Policy
    D. KMS Policies

Answer: A

Explanation: The main way in which Customer Master Keys (CMKs) are controlled in the AWS KMS is by key policies. This is a factor of control access without which, you cannot control the access.

149. You have a web application on AWS for your company who wants to disclose APIs that customers can invoke. You do not want to manage the underlying Web Service Infrastructure. Which two services would you like to use for this?
    A. AWS RDS
    B. AWS EC2
    C. AWS Lambda
    D. AWS API Gateway

Answer: C and D

Explanation: You can run code for almost any sort of implementation or backend service using Lambda — all with zero management. Just upload your code and Lambda will be responsible for running and scaling your code with high availability. You can automatically set your code to trigger from other AWS resources or call it from any web or mobile application.

Amazon API Gateway is a fully managed service that facilitates the creation, publication, maintenance, and security of developers' APIs at any scale. With just a few clicks on the AWS

management console, you can set up an API that acts as a "front gate" for apps using your backend services such as workloads operating on Amazon Elastic Compute Cloud (Amazon EC2), AWS Lambda code, or any web applications to access information, business logic or other features.

150. You have used a multi-tier Web Application for the deployment of a new application in the AWS. Web servers, application servers & database servers are implemented in the East region of the United States. Application Load Balancers are set to balance traffic across multiple AZs in the region for high availability. You use Amazon CloudFront at edge location in order to cache information. A blacklist IP address has been provided to the security team that is considered a spammer. You want to block IP addresses instantly at the farthest from the cloud infrastructure. What is the right choice for IP address blocking?

A. In the US East region, use Web ACL to block all IP address & apply it at Application Load Balancer

B. In the Global region, create Web ACL, to block all IP address & apply it at edge level CloudFront

C. In the US East region, create Web ACL, to block all IP address & apply it at edge level CloudFront

D. In each AZ of the US East region, create Web ACL to block all IP address & apply it at Application Load Balancer

Answer: B

Explanation: Use AWS WAF for blocking and detecting of IP addresses, Cross-Site scripting, SQL injection, pattern in HTTP header and body, geographical locations etc. This WAF AWS can be performed at the Amazon CloudFront edge location or ALB at the region level. Given that this Web ACL is needed at the farthest stage in the Web application, it must be applied at a global level at the edge location of Amazon CloudFront.

151. An enterprise is using EC2 instance along with EBS volume, and wants both root and data of every EBS volume to be retained even after the termination of instance. How would this be done?

A. By setting the DisableApiTermination attribute on the EC2 Instance to False

B. By setting the DisableApiTermination attribute on the EC2 Instance to True

C. By setting the DeleteOnTermination attribute for the volumes to False

D. By setting the DeletionOnTermination attribute for the volumes to True

Answer: C

Explanation: When an instance terminates, for each Amazon EBS volume attached, Amazon EC2 uses the value of the DeleteOnTermination attribute to determine whether to retain or delete the volume. By default, the root volume attribute of an instance is set to true. The default is, therefore, to delete an instance's root quantity when the instance ends.

152.   The SQS Queues for messaging are presently being used for your application architecture design. Your requirement is to guarantee the messages that are not processed effectively maintain a separate queue. For this purpose, what should you configure?
A. Dead Letter Queue
B. Queues with short polling
C. Delay Queues
D. FIFO Queues

Answer: A

Explanation: Amazon SQS supports dead-letter queues that can be used for messages that cannot effectively be processed (consumed). To debug your application or message scheme, dead letter queues are good because they allow you to isolate problem messages in order to determine why their processing was unsuccessful.

153.   An organization will need to perform penetration tests for EC2 instances. This must be done as part of the security process. In relation to penetration testing for EC2 instances, which of the following is TRUE?
A. It can be performed at any point in time
B. It can be performed by the customer on their own instances
C. It can be performed by AWS at certain times
D. It is not allowed under any circumstances

Answer: B

Explanation: Without any approval to perform a penetration test and security assessments, AWS allows its customer to do it at their own.

• Amazon EC2 instances, NAT gateways, and Elastic Load Balancers
• Amazon RDS
• Amazon CloudFront

- Amazon Aurora
- Amazon API Gateways
- AWS Lambda and Lambda Edge functions
- Amazon Lightsail resources
- Amazon Elastic Beanstalk environments

154. A company wants to allow its vendor to upload the files in S3 bucket without providing public access to the bucket. How will it do that?
   A. By providing an ElastiCache in front of the bucket
   B. By providing a CloudFront distribution in front of the bucket
   C. By creating a pre-signed URL for the S3 bucket
   D. By creating a bucket ACL to provide the required permission

Answer: C

Explanation: By default, every object and bucket is private. If the user or customer wants to be able to upload a certain object to your bucket, pre-signed URLs are useful, but you do not need AWS security credentials or permission for this. You must provide your security credentials when you generate your pre-signed URL and then indicate a bucket name, an item key, an HTTP technique (PUT for uploading objects) as well as expiry date and time. The pre-signed URLs are only valid for a specified period.

155. A company is using AWS S3 bucket to store critical data. It has deployed AWS Organization for managing all of its accounts. The contents of the bucket are only visible to the employees. But because of misconfiguration, the vendor's account out of the organization is also reachable to the contents. To prevent this problems, you were asked to create a strict policy and should also prevent adjustments to a policy when changing your accounts. Which of these criteria may comply with?
   A. Use aws:PrincipalOrgID condition key to match Organization ID & only allow members matching this ID to access S3 bucket
   B. Use s3:LocationConstraint key to match the location of members in an AWS organization & grant access to S3 bucket
   C. Use IAM Condition Key to match all accounts IDs to provide access to S3 bucket
   D. While specifying Resources in the policy statement, make sure only specific objects are granted access instead of allowing access to all objects in a folder

Answer: A

Explanation: You can use condition aws: PrincipalOrgID to match organization ID rather than account ID on many accounts to grant access to S3 bucket for AWS Organization employees. Users in the AWS organization will be granted this access, and all access to outside accounts (not within the AWS organization) will be refused.

156.   You need to publish metrics from several devices onto CloudWatch. There is a requirement to publish the metrics at an interval of 1 second. How can you accomplish this? (Choose 2)
   A. By publishing metrics with standard resolution
   B. By usng the AWS CLI to publish custom metrics
   C. By publishing metrics with high resolution
   D. By publishing custom metrics from the AWS Console

Answer: B and C

Explanation: Standard resolution is the default for the metrics generated by AWS services. You can identify a standard or high resolution metric by publishing a custom metric. CloudWatch stores a metric with a 1-second resolution when you publish a high-resolution, and it is available for reading and retrieval for 1 second, 5 seconds, 10 seconds, 30 seconds, or any 60-second multiple times.

157.   There are multiple CloudTrail log files that are defined by a company who now wants to make sure not a single file is being manipulated. How would this be done?
   A. By changing the bucket ACL for the log files to only allow read access
   B. By changing the IAM policy for the log files to only allow read access
   C. By changing the access for the log files to only allow read access
   D. By enabling log file integrity for the log files

Answer: D

Explanation: You can use CloudTrail log file integrity validation to establish whether a log file has been changed, deleted or unchanged after CloudTrail delivery. This function is made from industry standard algorithms: SHA-256 for hazing and SHA-256 for digital signing with RSA. This makes it computationally infeasible to modify, delete or forge CloudTrail log files without

detection. You can use the AWS CLI to validate the files in the location where CloudTrail delivered them.

158. An enterprise has its intranet apps include Hybrid infrastructure. On-premises users who use AD credentials to access AWS resources are complaining of re-logging after 1 hour of access. What could be the activities taken to prolong the user session?

A. Maximum User session duration that can be set with SAML is 1 hour
B. Use optional SAML attribute "SessionDuration" to set user session to a maximum of 12 hours
C. Use optional SAML attribute "SessionDuration" to set user session to a maximum of six hours
D. Remove SAML attribute "SessionDuration" so that it will have default User session duration of 12 hours

Answer: B

Explanation: SessionDuration is an optional SAML attribute to specify user session. The default can be 1 hour when no attributes are set. You can set a user session between 15 and 12 minutes.

159. An organization has its application which takes data from multiple IoT devices and writes it to DynamoDB table. There are 40 devices writing after every 10 sec. The size of individual data is 1 KB. What throughput for write can be assigned to the table?

A. 10 WCU
B. 12 WCU
C. 2 WCU
D. 4WCU

Answer: D

Explanation: As we calculated the number of writes per second, which is 40/10=4, we have to assign 4 WCU to the table.

160. A company is using VPN connection between VPC and on-premises network. Now it wants the instances in the VPC to resolve DNS name by using on-premises DNS server. How would this be done?

A. By modifying the DNS resolution of the VPC
B. By creating a DHCP Options set and assigning it to the VPC
C. By creating a secondary DNS server in AWS
D. By creating an Internal Route 53 hosted zone

Answer: B

Explanation: In the non-default VPC, Amazon EC2 instances that you launch are private, so public IPv4 addresses are not assigned if you do not specify it during launch or modify the public IPv4 subnet's address attribute. In a non-default VPC, all instances get an unsolvable host name assigned by AWS (ip-10-0-202, for instance) by default. You can allocate to your instance, your own domain name and use up to four of your own DNS servers. To do so, a special set of DHCP options must be specified for use with the VPC.

161. An enterprise wants to present some metrics for monitoring the following:
   - Network Throughput into the EC2 Instances
   - Amount of Disk storage left on the volume
   - CPU Utilization for the underlying EC2 Instances
   - Number of bytes read and written to the volume

Which one of the above needs a custom CloudWatch metric?

A. The amount of Disk storage left on the volume
B. The number of bytes read and written to the volume
C. CPU Utilization for the underlying EC2 Instances
D. Network Throughput into the EC2 Instances

Answer: A

Explanation: In CloudWatch, the available metrics are: CPU utilization, Volume Read and Write and Network throughput. So for the amount of disk storage left on volume, you will need a custom metric for monitoring.

162. An enterprise has a set of EC2 instances that sits behind an ELB. These instances are hosting a web server. When the enterprise tries to reach to the web page of the webserver via ELB, it is unable to do that. But when reaching the webserver on the EC2 Instance itself via a bastion host, it works. Which of the following needs to be checked when you are unable to connect via ELB? (Choose 2)

A. Ensure that access logging is enabled for the ELB
B. Ensure that the ELB is attached to a private subnet
C. Ensure that the ELB security group allows Inbound Traffic
D. Ensure that the ELB is attached to a public subnet

Answer: C and D

Explanation: When your ELB, which is internet facing, is unable to respond to the request, check the following:

- ELB must be in public subnet
- Security group and NACL must allow inbound and outbound traffic to and from the client on listener port

163.   A company has its application hosted on sites across multiple regions. Now the users want to be directed to the site on the basis of minimum time of reachability. How would this be done?
A. By using Route 53 with latency-based routing
B. By using the Network Load balancer with an Elastic IP
C. By using Route 53 with weighted-based routing
D. By using the Application Load balancer with path-based routing

Answer: A

Explanation: For the application running multiple regions, the performance can be improved by serving a request from the region that gives least latency. By using Route 53 latency-based routing, you can create latency records for your resources in multiple AWS regions. If Route 53 gets a DNS query on your domain or subdomain (example.com or apex.example.com), it determines what region of AWS you have created, gives the user the lowest latency, and chooses a latency record for that region. Route 53 responds to the value of the selected record, like the webserver IP address.

164.   Your application is running on an EC2 instance, which is one of the critical applications. In case the primary instance goes down, you want it to be easily shifted to another EC2 instance. The AMI of the primary instance is also taken for launching a secondary instance. How would you shift the application smoothly to the secondary instance?
A. By creating a secondary NAT gateway for the VPC

B. By creating a secondary internet gateway for the VPC

C. By assigning an Elastic IP to the primary instance

D. By assigning a secondary ENI to the primary instance

Answer: C

Explanation: The Elastic IP address can be disconnected from the resource and re-associated to a separate resource. Even after you disassociate its Elastic IP address and associate it with another instance, any open connections to an instance remain working for the moment. These links should be reopened using the re-associated Elastic IP address.

165. A vendor-based product must be hosted on an EC2 instance. Due to the nature of the product licensing model, the number of cores of the underlying hardware should be controlled by you. In that situation, what would you take into account?

A. Dedicated Hosts

B. Reserved Instances

C. Dedicated Instances

D. Spot Instances

Answer: A

Explanation: You may run the Amazon EC2 instances on a physical server dedicated to your use with dedicated hosts and instances. An important difference between a dedicated host and a dedicated instance is that a dedicated host gives you additional visibility and control of how instances are placed on a physical server and that you can always use the same physical server over time to deploy your instances. The dedicated hosting systems, therefore, enable you to use your existing server-binding software licenses and meet company compliance and regulatory requirements.

166. A company is using MySQL instance on AWS RDS and needs to know which activity would be required in a maintenance window. How would this be done? (Choose 3)

A. By creating an Options group for the database

B. By applying Patches to the server

C. By updating the underlying Operating System

D. By changing the underlying DB version

Answer: B, C and D

Explanation: Amazon RDS regularly conducts maintenance on RDS assets from Amazon. Most often, maintenance includes updates to the underlying OS (OS) or database version of the DB instance/DB cluster. Operating system updates should be done more frequently to avoid safety problems.

167. You have an application that is hosted on a set of EC2 instances. These instances are behind an Elastic Load Balancer. You want that Route 53 is configured with Company's Domain name to the Elastic Load Balancer. Which record would you produce for this purpose?

A. AAAA Record
B. MX Record
C. A Record
D. ALIAS Record

Answer: D

Explanation: The Amazon Route 53 alias records are an extension of the DNS functionality on Route 53–Specific extension. Alias records allow you to route traffic on selected AWS resources such as CloudFront and Amazon S3 buckets. If Route 53 receives an alias record's DNS query, it answers for the resource with the relevant value:

- An Amazon API Gateway custom regional API or edge-optimized API
- A CloudFront distribution
- An ELB load balancer
- Another Route 53 record in the same hosted zone
- An Amazon VPC interface endpoint
- An Elastic Beanstalk environment
- An Amazon S3 bucket that is configured as a static website

168. A company is using CloudFormation template for spinning up the resources as per requirement. The template must be flexible for values based on the region where the template has been launched. Which section in the template is helpful for this requirement?

A. Mappings
B. Resources
C. Conditions
D. Outputs

Answer: A

Explanation: The Mapping section coincides with a key for the corresponding set of named values. For example, if you want to set values based on a region, a mapping can be created that uses the region's name as a key and contains the values for each particular region defined by you. You use the intrinsic function "Fn::FindInMap" to find values in the map.

169.   An application is using Aurora MySQL database. Because of an increase in Read workload, you want to create ReadReplica in a different region. Which of the following can be used for cross region replica?

A. Amazon Aurora MySQL automatically creates a cross-region Read Replica for Amazon Aurora MySQL DB cluster

B. Amazon Aurora MySQL only supports in-region replica & not a cross-region replica

C. Up to 5 cross-region Read-Replica is supported for both encrypted & unencrypted DB cluster in any AWS region

D. Up to 5 cross-region Read-Replica are supported for only unencrypted DB cluster in any AWS region

Answer: C

Explanation: Read Replicas can be generated for Amazon Aurora MySQL database to boost the accessibility and allow users to improve reading efficiency by reading information from the closest regions. For both encrypted and unencrypted DB clusters in various AWS regions, up to 5 read replicas can be created. The AWS Management Console, AWS CLI, or the Amazon RDS API can create these cross-region Read Replicas.

170.   A financial institute has critical files that are accessed frequently in the beginning, but now are hardly accessed. By keeping in mind that the cost should be minimum, which one is the best option for these files?

A. Store the files on Amazon Glacier and then use lifecycle policies to copy the files to Amazon S3

B. Store the files on S3 and then use lifecycle policies to copy the files to Amazon Glacier

C. Store the files on EBS volumes and then use lifecycle policies to copy the files to Amazon Glacier

D. Store the files on EBS volumes and then use lifecycle policies to create snapshots

Answer: B

Explanation: Configure your life cycle to handle your objects, so they are stored economically during your lifecycle. A lifecycle configuration is a set of rules that define actions for a group of objects that apply with Amazon S3. There are two actions:

- **Transition Action:** It is defined for the transition of an object to another storage class
- **Expiration Action:** It is defined to delete an expired object on your behalf

171. Your company uses AWS resources and, as part of the policy on business continuity, you need to ensure that all resources are backed up. AWS performs automated backups on which of the following resources? (Choose 3)
   A. AWS RDS
   B. AWS EC2
   C. AWS Redshift
   D. AWS EBS

Answer: A, C and D

Explanation: Amazon RDS will create and save your DB instance's automated backups. Amazon RDS provides a DB instance, snapshot storage volume that supports a full DB instance rather than a single database.

Amazon Redshift regularly takes snapshots of that cluster, generally every eight hours or after every 5 GB of information changing per node or whoever arrives first, if automated snapshots are activated for a cluster. When creating a cluster, automated snapshots can be activated by default. At the end of a retention period, these snapshots are deleted. Default retention time is one day, but the Amazon Redshift console or the Amazon Redshift API allows you to change it programmatically.

172. An enterprise has MySQL databases on premises, which now need to be moved to AWS. The enterprise does not want to worry about the scaling and operating of the database when moving to AWS. How can this be done?
   A. AWS RDS
   B. AWS Aurora
   C. AWS Redshift
   D. AWS DynamoDB

Answer: B

Explanation: Aurora makes the setup, operation and scaling of your MySQL and PostgreSQL deployments easy and affordable, allowing you to concentrate on your company and apps. Amazon RDS offers management for Aurora, including provisioning, patching, back up, restoration, failure detection and repair, by managing daily routine database tasks. The pushbutton migration tools from Amazon RDS are also provided to convert your current Amazon RDS MySQL or Postgre SQL to Aurora.

173.   You are new to AWS, and you want to understand the actions you need to perform by yourself and the ones done for you by AWS. From the following, which are done by AWS? (Choose 2)

    A. Getting compliance documents from AWS to get a breakdown of the physical infrastructure

    B. Requesting for increase in the number of load balancers per region

    C. Getting a consolidated bill for all of the accounts you own

    D. Requesting for increase in the number of DynamoDB tables per account more than allocated by default

Answer: B and D

Explanation: There are service limits of multiple resources that AWS gives. You need to contact AWS to request an increase if you exceed the limit.

174.   An enterprise is using AWS and wants to keep track of the cost of all resources and get billing alerts. Before receiving billing alerts, what must be enabled in AWS?

    A. Request an AWS support partner to notify you on estimated charges

    B. Request AWS support to notify you on estimated charges

    C. Enable billing alerts in Account Preferences

    D. Enable billing alerts in CloudWatch

Answer: C

Explanation: You must enable the billing alerts before creating an alarm for estimated charges. After that, you can monitor the estimated charges and create an alarm on billing metric data. Once billing alerts are enabled, they cannot be disabled, but you can delete the alarms that you created.

175.   You have an EC2-EBS-backed Linux instance on which an application is running. After some time, you realize that you lost its private key and are able to login to the instance. What can you do in this scenario? (Choose 2)

   A.   Use another private key to log into the instance
   B.   Modify the authorized_keys file on the volume
   C.   Detach the root volume from the instance and attach it to another instance
   D.   Terminate the instance and create a new one

Answer: B and C

Explanation: You can regain access to your instance by losing your private key for an EBS-backed instance. You must stop it, detach its root volume, and add it as information volume to another instance, edit the authorized_keys file, transfer the volume back to the instance and restart the instance.

176.   The AutoScaling Group and the Elastic Load Balancer were created by your team. As part of the AutoScaling Group, the instances launched are connected to the Elastic Load Balancer. A number of users exercising the application noted that traffic is not equally distributed throughout the EC2 instances. Which of the following may be the reasons? (Choose 2)

   A.   The subnets that host the EC2 Instances are private subnets
   B.   All regions that have the EC2 Instances have not been registered with the load balancer
   C.   All subnets that have the EC2 Instances have not been registered with the load balancer
   D.   Sticky sessions have been enabled for the load balancer

Answer: C and D

Explanation: Choose the subnets from the same AZs as your instances. If you have an internet-facing load balancer, you must choose public subnets to receive load balancer traffic for your back-end applications.

The Classic Load Balancer routes each application with the lowest load by default to the registered instance. However, the sticky session function (also known as the session affinity) can be used to connect the load balancer to a particular instance, so that all user requests are sent in a single instance during this session.

177.   A financial company wants to migrate some of its databases to AWS. This includes Oracle 10g Release 2 and MySQL v5.6 based workloads. There are applications that are connected to

these databases and are read intensively for which the company decides to use AWS RDS Read Replica's feature. What issue might they face during this architecture implementation?

A. Read Replicas are not supported with the given version of Oracle
B. You cannot migrate an Oracle workload to AWS
C. You need to enable the Multi-AZ option for Read Replicas
D. Read replicas are not supported with MySQL v5.6

Answer: A

Explanation: Amazon RDS started supporting Oracle from the version 12.1.0.2.v10 and higher 12.1 versions, and for all 12.2 versions. RDS Read Replicas provide improved database (DB) performance and durability. This function facilitates the elastic scale of the read-heavy database workload over the capacities of a single DB instance. You can create one or more replicas for a certain source DB instance and use these multiple copies of your data to serve high volume read-traffic applications to increase the aggregate read performance. If you are required to make a standalone DB instance, replicas can also be promoted. Amazon RDS, MariaDB, PostgreSQL and Oracle as well as Amazon Aurora also have Read replicas.

178. An application hosted in AWS is using the AWS RDS service. The database is MySQL. Now, some performance problems are noticed in the application. After some more investigation on the issue, it was observed that the database is overloaded and cannot handle the amount of read request. Which one of the following can be implemented to resolve the database performance issue? (Choose 2)

A. Enable Multi-AZ for the database
B. Add a Read Replica for the database
C. Add a CloudFront distribution in front of the load balancer
D. Increase the Instance type for the underlying database server

Answer: B and D

Explanation: For intensive read workload, you can add Read Replica for the database that is horizontal scaling. RDS MySQL, PostgreSQL, and MariaDB can have up to 5 read replicas, and Amazon Aurora can have up to 15 read replicas. You can perform scaling of the database by vertical scaling in which you can change the size of the instance.

179. A company plans to deploy its application server on AWS and the critical server in VPC. The company's security team is looking for a consolidated list of all connections that are made

to the SSH ports, to further improve the security groups attached to these servers. How will this be done?

A. By using Amazon Athena to query S3 bucket with VPC flow logs saved

B. By exporting VPC logs to S3 buckets & using S3 Analytics to analyze log files

C. By using third party tools to query VPC logs saved in an S3 bucket

D. By exporting VPC flow logs into CSV format & filtering based upon SSH port 22

Answer: A

Explanation: The VPC flow log can be saved into an S3 bucket once VPC flow logo is enabled. You can use Amazon Athena to query this data from any VPC Flow Logs' table field. No further infrastructure needs to be established with Amazon Athena, and pricing is only based on the number of queries of a data in S3 buckets.

180. An enterprise has a set of EC2 Instances in a VPC. A mountable file storage system is required, which can be used and shared with EC2 instances. Which of the following services should be used for this need?

A. AWS EBS

B. AWS Glacier

C. AWS EFS

D. AWS S3

Answer: C

Explanation: For use with Amazon EC2, Amazon EFS offers scalable file storage. You can build an EFS file system and configure an instance for mounting the file system. For workloads and applications running on multiple instances, you can use an EFS file system as a common data source.

181. Your business has launched a number of AWS resources. A security mandate is now in place to ensure all changes in resources are monitored. Which one of the following services can help you with your requirement? (Choose 2)

A. AWS Config

B. AWS Trusted Advisor

C. AWS CloudWatch

D. AWS CloudTrail

Answer: A and D

Explanation: AWS Config is a service that allows you to asses, audit and evaluate your AWS resources configuration. With AWS Config, you can continuously monitor and record the AWS resource configurations, and you can automatically evaluate recorded configurations against the desired configurations. Config enables you to review changes to AWS resources configurations and relationships between resource.

AWS CloudTrail is a service to govern, adhere to and audit your AWS account operation and risk. You can log, continuously monitor and retain your AWS infrastructure account activity with CloudTrail. CloudTrail provides the AWS account event history including the measures taken via the AWS Management Console, AWS SDKs, tools for the command line and any other AWS services. It simplifies security analysis, tracking and troubleshooting of the change of resource.

182. You work as a SysOps administrator for an IT company with an IT server infrastructure in AWS Cloud. Recently, a start-up company was acquired and needs to share project data saved in EFS with the start-up company. This data is accessed by users from a company who are working on Linux servers. Which is the safest and most feasible option for granting this company access?

A. Create a Mount target with a security group allowing outbound TCP protocol on NFS port to start-up company on-prem Linux servers over the internet

B. Create a Mount target with a security group allowing outbound TCP protocol on NFS port to start-up company on-prem Linux servers over AWS Direct Connect

C. Create a Mount target with a security group allowing inbound TCP protocol on NFS port from start-up company on-prem Linux servers over the internet

D. Create a Mount target with a security group allowing inbound TCP protocol on NFS port from start-up company on-prem Linux servers over AWS Direct Connect

Answer: D

Explanation: You can access the EFS mount targets from EC2 instance in local VPC, On-premises servers that have VPN or Direct Connect connection to VPC and EC2 instance in VPC peered with other VPCs. Also, the Mount Objective Security Group should enable inbound NFS port connectivity from on-prem servers, and all those servers should have an outbound policy to enable mount target access on the NFS port.

183. A company has set NACL rule for its VPC. The first rule is Rule#100, which denies all traffic on all ports. The second rule is Rule#105, which allows HTTP traffic with TCP protocol on port 80 from anywhere. From the below following statement, which one is true?
    A. All traffic out of the subnet will be denied
    B. All traffic on all ports will not be allowed to flow into the subnet
    C. A request from a workstation on the Internet with IP address 52.10.1.2 will be allowed onto the EC2 Instance on port 80
    D. There will be an error in setting the rules for the Security Group rules due to the clash in rules

Answer: B

Explanation: The rule that has rule#100 will be evaluated first, so it denies all traffic into the subnet.

184. The company has a range of AWS tools. Your senior management does not support the recent proposal for the use of AWS assets and has asked you to reduce costs as far as possible. Which can prove to be benefit in this cause from the following? (Choose 3)
    A. Consider terminating EC2 Instances that are not being used
    B. Consider not using AutoScaling Group as they incur a cost
    C. Consider deleting EBS volumes that are not attached to EC2 Instances and are not being used
    D. Consider purchasing reserved instances for those workloads that run continuously and on a daily basis

Answer: A, C and D

Explanation: The Amazon EC2 Reserved Instances (RIs) provide a substantial (up to 75%) advantage over on-demand pricing and offer resource reservations for use in a particular area of availability.

You can also delete the instance that is not in use because stop instances also incur charges. EBS volumes, if not connected to the instance, also incur charges. So, after taking a snapshot of a volume, delete the EBS volume to save cost.

185.   An enterprise is looking for an audit of AWS resources and is requesting for the compliance of AWS resources to various compliance standards. How could the enterprise go about working towards these compliance details?

   A. By going to the compliance portion of the AWS website and getting all the required details
   B. By requesting an AWS partner for all compliance-based documents
   C. By requesting AWS support for all compliance-based documents
   D. By requesting a tour of the AWS physical data center from AWS support

Answer: A

Explanation: To get all detail about the compliance document, you can go to the AWS website's compliance portion.

186.   A blog posting company host its application in which some of your posts are static in nature. Because of a large number of hits, the application becomes slow. Which of the following can be used to reduce the problem of many users who have hit these pages on the application?

   A. Consider using the latency policy in Route 53
   B. Consider creating a Read Replica of the database
   C. Consider placing ElastiCache in front of the database
   D. Consider hosting the web pages using static web site hosting in S3

Answer: D

Explanation: In Amazon S3, you can host a static website. There is a static content on a static website and might contain client-side scripts. On the other hand, a dynamic website use server-side processing, including server-side scripts such as PHP, JSP, or ASP.NET. Amazon S3 does not support server-side scripting. To host dynamic website in AWS, there are resources available.

187.   A big IT company manages different accounts in various regions using AWS Organization. All AWS Cost & Usage documents are stored in CSV format in an S3. As an administrator, you have been assigned with the task of querying these reports via Amazon Athena. What can be used to define the bucket path in Amazon Athena?

   A. arn:aws:s3:::bucketname/prefix/
   B. s3://bucketname/prefix/
   C. s3://bucketname/prefix/*

D. s3.amazon.com/bucketname/prefix/

Answer: B

Explanation: You can define the path of data to be read using LOCATION property when building a table in Amazon Athena. This is the path "s3:/bucketname / prefix/" and Amazon Athena reads all of the data stored here.

188.   Currently, a firm is hosting an application on EC2 instances. As part of an AutoScaling Group, these EC2 instances are being launched. During office hours, (from 8-4) the application is extensively used. Users complain that the application is performing slowly at the beginning of the day, and after that, the application is working properly. What can be done to make sure the application works correctly at the start of the day?

A. Add an Application Load balancer to the entire setup
B. Add a Dynamic scaling policy for the AutoScaling Group to launch new instances based on the CPU utilization
C. Add a Scheduled scaling policy for the AutoScaling Group to launch new instances before the start of the day
D. Add a Dynamic scaling policy for the AutoScaling Group to launch new instances based on the Memory utilization

Answer: C

Explanation: The best option here is to make sure that the instances are already scaled up and ready to use before the day begins. So, we should use scheduled scaling policy in AutoScaling Group for the betterment of the performance.

189.   A company is using Memcached cluster and observes that a large amount of data is rejected on recent CloudWatch metric data. How would the company mitigate the increased amount of rejection? (Choose 2)

A. By restarting the cluster
B. By increasing the node size
C. By changing the underlying volume for the cluster to use Provisioned IOPS
D. By adding an additional node to the cluster

Answer: B and D

Explanation: If your requests are rejected with your cluster, it usually represents a sign that you must scale up (use a node with larger memory footprints) or scale out (include additional cluster nodes). An exception to this rule is when you use the cache engine to handle your keys by eviction, which also is referred to as an LRU cache.

190. A company has an application for which it uses the AutoScaling Group to launch instances. Lately, the launching of instance is failing, and the company wants to debug the issue. From the following, what may be the reason behind the failure? (Choose 3)
    A. The instance type is no longer available
    B. The wrong NACL has been specified
    C. The key pair associated with the instance does not exist
    D. The requested Availability Zone is no longer supported

Answer: A, C and D

Explanation: When an instance launch fails, then the following may be the reasons:
- The security group <name of the security group> does not exist
- The key pair <key pair associated with your EC2 instance> does not exist. The requested configuration is currently not supported
- AutoScalingGroup <Auto Scaling group name> not found
- The requested Availability Zone is no longer supported
- Your requested instance type (<instance type>) is not supported in your requested Availability Zone (<instance Availability Zone>)
- You are not subscribed to this service
- Invalid device name upload
- Value (<name associated with the instance storage device>) for parameter virtualName is invalid
- EBS block device mappings not supported for instance-store AMIs
- Placement groups may not be used with instances of type 'm1.large'
- Client.InternalError: Client error on launch

191. Your organization has an application pre-requisite to begin instances. There should be a low latency between the instances and a high packet network performance. What will you do to ensure that these conditions are fulfilled? (Choose 2)
    A. Choose a GPU optimized instance type for the underlying instance

B. Choose an instance type that supports Enhanced Networking for the underlying instance type
C. Create a cluster placement group grouping the instances in a single availability zone
D. Create a cluster placement group grouping the instances in multiple availability zones

Answer: B and C

Explanation: A cluster placement group is a logical group of instances in a single AZ. For applications that are benefitting from low network latency, high network bandwidth, or both, cluster placement groups are suggested if most of the network traffic is between instances. Choose a type of instance that supports enhanced networking to offer the lowest latency and highest network per second for the placement group.

192.   You are using AutoScaling Group to launch instances, but now you want to change the instance type of running instances and also want that when ASG launch the instance, it belongs to a new type. How would you do this? (Choose 2)
A. By modifying the existing launch configuration
B. By modifying the AutoScaling Group with the modified launch configuration
C. By modifying the AutoScaling Group with the new launch configuration
D. By creating a new launch configuration

Answer: C and D

Explanation: With multiple Auto Scaling groups, you can specify launch configuration. But the launch configuration cannot be modified after the creation of ASG. There is only one launch configuration at a time. So, to change the launch configuration, you need to create a configuration and update ASG with this new configuration.

193.   A company is using a number of instances and EBS volumes. If a primary region goes down, the company wants its EBS volume to be available in another region. How can this be done?
A. By creating a snapshot and copying the snapshot to the new region.
B. By creating a copy of the volume and copying the volume to the new region
C. By creating a snapshot from the volume in another region
D. By creating a copy of the volume in another region

Answer: A

Explanation: You can create point-in-time snapshots of volumes with Amazon EBS and AWS stores it in Amazon S3. After the snapshot is completed, you can copy it from an AWS region to another or the same region.

194.   An instance is launched by an organization in its custom VPC, but the instance is not getting public DNS. What might be the reason for this? (Choose 2)
   A. The route tables have not been modified to include the Internet gateway
   B. enableDnsHostNames is set to No
   C. There is no Internet gateway attached to the VPC
   D. enableDnsSupport is set to No

Answer: B and D

Explanation: For an instance to get the public DNS name, you need the attribute values to be true. One is enableDnsHostnames and second is enableDnsSupport. If any one or both of them is false, then the instance having Public IP did not get the DNS hostnames and Amazon-provided DNS server cannot resolve Amazon-provided private DNS hostnames. By default, both values are true.

195.   You are planning to use AWS RDS service for hosting databases. You require all traffic to be encrypted at rest. How can you do this?
   A. By using the KMS service to encrypt the traffic
   B. By using the SSL certificates provided by the AWS RDS service
   C. By using the .pem keys files that come for the underlying server
   D. By using the .ppk key files that comes from the underlying server

Answer: B

Explanation: You can use SSL to encrypt links between your server applications and Microsoft SQL Server running Amazon RDS Database instances. For all supported SQL Server versions, SSL support is available in all AWS regions.

Amazon RDS creates SSL certificates for a SQL Server DB instance. The SSL certificate includes the DB instance endpoint as the SSL certificate's Common Name (CN) to defend against spoofing.

196. An enterprise uses CloudFormation to create stacks, and during creation, it wants all occurring errors to be corrected manually. How can this be done?
    A. By setting the ForceAPI for the stack as DO_NOT_DELETE
    B. By enabling Termination protection on the stack
    C. By setting the OnFailure to DO_NOTHING when creating the stack
    D. By setting the DeleteAPI for the stack to None

Answer: C

Explanation: By default, if stack creation fails, then it will rollback. However, as manual error resolving is required, set OnFailure attribute to DO_NOTHING. In this way, failure in creation allows you to correct errors manually.

197. A financial sector has a number of servers on its on-premises locations. These servers are Windows 2012 with limitation on usage of storage. To provide further storage, AWS is being planned to be used. NTFS file permissions are needed for the volumes for these servers. Which storage option should be chosen to meet the requirement? (Choose 2)
    A. AWS Storage Volume Gateway
    B. AWS EFS
    C. AWS S3
    D. AWS Storage File Gateway

Answer: A and D

Explanation: You can use storage file gateway and volume gateway as a storage service for on-premises servers. The SMB (Service Message Block) protocol has been introduced to File Gateway by AWS Storage Gateway, which allows file-based applications by Microsoft Windows using S3 to store and access object conveniently. The volume gateway with NTFS file permissions can be used to create the volumes.

198. You have an EC2 Instance fleet and need a shared data store. The products will be between 1 KB and 300 MB in length. The data store will have a maximum size of 3 TB. The data needs to have a consistent read view. Few changes are made to the information with no conflicts. What is best data storage for this requirement from the following?
    A. AWS S3
    B. AWS EFS

C. AWS DynamoDB

D. AWS EBS Volume

Answer: B

Explanation: Amazon EFS file systems can scale automatically from gigabytes to petabytes of data without processing. Tens or thousands of instances of Amazon EC2 can access an Amazon EFS file system simultaneously, and each Amazon EC2 instance is provided with consistent performance.

199. A company has a large number of EBS snapshot that is used for the recovery of an EBS volume. Now, the company wants the snapshots older than six months that are not required anymore to be deleted. How can this be done in the easiest way possible? (Choose 2)

   A. By creating an Elastic Beanstalk environment and setting up a cron job to delete EBS snapshots older than six months

   B. By using Step Functions and CloudWatch events to schedule the deletion of older EBS snapshots

   C. By creating an EC2 Instance and setting up a cron job to delete EBS snapshots older than six months

   D. By using Amazon Data Lifecycle Manager to delete the old snapshots

Answer: B and D

Explanation: The creation, deletion and retention of snapshots automatically can be done via Amazon Data Lifecycle Manager. According to schedule, you can run CloudWatch events rule. You can create an automatic snapshot of a current Amazon EBS volume. A fixed rate can be used to produce a snapshot after every few minutes or to indicate that the snapshot is created at a particular time of the days via a cron job.

200. AMI from an EC2 instance was recently created by your team. You have to share this with a different account that is held by the same company. What is the best way to ensure that the AMI will be accessible to the other account?

   A. Sharing the AMI with the specific AWS account

   B. Selling the AMI in the AWS Marketplace

   C. Making the AMI as a paid AMI

   D. Marking the AMI as public

Answer: A

Explanation: You can share an AMI with specific AWS accounts without making the AMI public. You just need the AWS IDs. AMI is only available in that region because it is a regional source. If you want to make an AMI available in another region, copy it into another region and then share it.

201.   You have an application that has the following requirements:
- Use AWS RDS for backend relational database
- Use EC2 instances for the web tier
- Load balancer for traffic distribution
- NAT gateway for traffic routing to the internet from database

What can be used from the following to increase the availability and scalability? (Choose 2)
A. Use Route 53 instead of the Load balancer
B. Launch the EC2 Instances as part of an AutoScaling Group
C. Enable Multi-AZ for the database
D. Use a NAT Instance instead of a NAT gateway

Answer: B and C

Explanation: Amazon EC2, Auto Scaling helps to ensure that you are able to handle your application load with the right number of Amazon EC2 Instances. You must build a set of EC2 instance called Auto Scaling Groups. In this, you can specify the minimum number of instance, of which you do not want your group to go down. Similarly, you can specify the number of maximum instance for the upper limit of the group.

Multiple AZ deployments from Amazon RDS provide improved database flexibility and durability so that they fit naturally to the workloads of production databases. Amazon RDS automatically creates a primary DB instance when providing a Multi-AZ DB instance and replicates data synchronically into a backup instance in another AZ.

202.   A company is using a large number of resources in AWS, and observe in audit, that EC2 instances have many unused Elastic IPs. From the following, which is the best tool for cost improvement?
A. AWS Inspector
B. AWS Systems Manager

C. AWS Trusted Advisor

D. AWS Config

Answer: C

Explanation: By using AWS Trusted Advisor, you can save AWS costs by eliminating unused or idle resources and making reserved capacity commitments.

203. An enterprise has an EC2 Instance that has general purpose SSD volume. Capacity size is 6. The number of IOPS needs to be augmented. How would this be done? (Choose 2)

A. By placing the volume in a RAID 0 configuration

B. By placing the volume in a RAID 1 configuration

C. By increasing the size of the volume

D. By changing the volume to Provisioned IOPS

Answer: A and D

Explanation: An io1 volume can range in size from 4 GiB to 16 TiB, and you can provision 100 up to 32,000 IOPS per volume. The maximum IOPS for a General Purpose SSD is 16,000. RAID 0 can strip multiple volumes together to increase the I / O quality than with a single volume, and RAID 1 can mirror two volumes together for the on-instance redundancy.

204. There is a variety of AWS tools being used by a media company. An array of DynamoDB tables is one of them. The requests made on the DynamoDB table are facing latency that needs to be reduced. What can be used for this requirement?

A. DynamoDB Streams

B. Secondary Indexes

C. DAX

D. Global Tables

Answer: C

Explanation: Amazon DynamoDB Accelerator (DAX) is a fully controlled, highly available DynamoDB in-Memory cache that improves performance up to 10 times from milliseconds to microseconds, even for millions of requests per second. DAX takes all the lifts needed to add in-memory acceleration to your DynamoDB tables without the developers needing to manage invalidation of the cache population of information or the management of clusters.

205.   AWS CloudHSM is used for SSL/TLS support along with web servers. There was an incident in which a user removed a key that affected the webserver from AWS CloudHSM. The Security Team Lead reviews AWS CloudHSM logs and identifies people who initiated commands to delete AWS CloudHSM keys. Since this is an AWS CloudHSM live, lots of logs are created each minute. In which of the following fields in AWS CloudHSM will the exact command be found that is used by the user for the key deletion?

A. Opcode
B. Session Handle
C. Command Type
D. Response

Answer: A

Explanation: There are multiple fields defined in AWS CloudHSM audit log for example:

Time: 12/19/17 21:01:17.140812, usecs:1513717277140812

Sequence No: 0x1

Reboot counter: 0xe8

Command Type(hex): CN_MGMT_CMD (0x0)

Opcode: CN_GEN_PSWD_ENC_KEY (0x1d)

Session Handle: 0x1004001

Response: 0:HSM Return: SUCCESS

Log type: MINIMAL_LOG_ENTRY (0)

In this, Opcode defines management commands which were executed. So, CN_DESTROY_OBJECT (0x11) command is used for deletion of a key if it is present in the log.

206.   An enterprise wants to host its systems on AWS. The systems need to be up and running even with a few glitches. In case of any issues with the underlying hardware hosting AWS services, the company must be informed. Which of the following can help to achieve this?

A. AWS CloudTrail Tool
B. AWS Config Tool
C. AWS Trusted Advisor Tool
D. Personal Health Dashboard

Answer: D

Explanation: AWS Personal Health Dashboard offers warnings and feedbacks if AWS has activities that could impact you. As a general state of AWS services is displayed from the Service Health Dashboard, Personal Health Dashboard provides a personal look at the availability and performance of AWS services that are underlying your AWS resources. The dashboard shows accurate and appropriate data to assist you in running events and provides constructive notification for scheduling activities. The Personal Health Dashboard gives you information and knowledge on how to treat problems easily by alerting changes in the health of AWS resources.

207.   The AWS database is managed by a company. The local department wants to whitelist the request according to IP/s. What is the AWS component/feature that makes the IP Address whitelisting perfect for the company?

A. AWS Route 53
B. AWS Network Load Balancer
C. AWS Application Load Balancer
D. AWS Classic Load balancer

Answer: B

Explanation: A layer 4 TCP load balancer was termed as the Network Load Balancer (NLB). For each availability zone, NLB requires static IP addresses. The static addresses do not alter. Therefore, they are perfect for the whitelisting of firewalls. NLB does not require HTTPS to be downloaded. However, it works only for TCP protocol.

208.   A webserver is deployed on EC2 instance with the domain name as example.org. Because of a large number of subdomain creation, while creating these certificates using Amazon Certificate Manager, you are planning to use wildcard name with the domain. Which of the following are valid Domain Names that will be supported using an ACM certificate with wildcard *.example.org? (Choose 2)

A. error.login.example.org
B. example.org
C. login.example.org
D. example.com
E. abc.example.org

Answer: C and E

Explanation: ACM supports wild card name while creating certificates. With an Asterix (*) in the leftmost part of the domain, it supports any subdomain up to 1 level. In the above case, wildcard *.example.org will protect following sub-domains abc.example.org & login.example.org. It will not protect an apex domain example.org & two levels of sub-domain.

209. An organization has been using a personalized approach to handle the tapes. An incident occurred because of which tapes are not available. AWS is now to be used by the organization to prevent this problem in the future. In this relation, which of these would be an ideal solution?

   A. Using AWS Storage Gateway as a VTL for cloud backup
   B. Storing all the tape data in Amazon Simple Storage Service
   C. Storing all the tape data in Amazon Glacier
   D. Storing all the tape data on EBS volumes

Answer: A

Explanation: In addition to providing trustworthy backup resources, AWS Storage Gateway provides IT organizations a streamlined way to move backup jobs from tape or Virtual Tape Library to the cloud. It reduces manual effort and gains predictable retrieval times.

210. An educational institute uses RDS instance as a database server that needs to be connected to the instance on which application is hosting. But the error "Error connecting to database" is observed. After complete verification, the institute is able to connect to the database from Bastion host which is in Public subnet. What could be the possible reason behind this error? (Choose any 2)

   A. The database server has the wrong ingress Security group rule for the web server
   B. The certificate used by the web server is not recognized by the database server
   C. The application is using the wrong port number in the connection string
   D. The database server has the wrong egress security group rule for the web server

Answer: A and C

Explanation: The reasons behind the inability to access the DB are:

   • There is no match between the access rules imposed by your local firewall and the IP addresses you allowed in the instance security group to access your DB instance. The

problem is probably your security group's ingress rule. The access is not allowed by DB instances by default; a security group is used to give access. You should build your own security group with specific rules of ingress and egress for your situation in order to allow access

- According to your firewall restrictions, the port you specified during the development of the DB instance cannot be used for sending or receiving communication. In this case, consult with your network administrator to see if the port you want to use for inbound and outbound communication can be accessed from your network
- The instance may still be is in creating state because of size, so it can take a few minutes

211. A mobile development company develops a mobile application. The mobile application clients must be capable of logging in and using AWS resources. Which of the following services would you use to fulfill this requirement? (Choose 2)

A. AWS IAM Users
B. AWS IAM Roles
C. AWS Cognito
D. AWS Federated Access

Answer: B and C

Explanation: Amazon Cognito identity pools grant temporary, restricted privilege access to your AWS services to your authenticated users. The permissions are managed for each user through IAM roles you create. You may set rules for selecting the position of each user on the basis of the user's ID token claims. For authenticated users, you can define a default role. Also, a separate IAM role can be specified with restricted permissions for non-authenticated guest users.

212. A company is using AutoScaling group from which some EC2 instances are launched. Now, they have seen that few new instances of EC2 are not counted for the Auto Scaling group's aggregated metrics. What could be the best possible reason for this?

A. The wrong launch configuration has been used
B. The instances have not been attached to the AutoScaling Group
C. The instances have not completed their boot sequence
D. The warm period has not expired

Answer: D

Explanation: You may specify the number of seconds you need to warm up with a newly started instance by using step scale policies. The instance is not measured according to the aggregated AutoScaling group metrics until its warming period expires.

213. A company would like to switch a JSON-based data store to AWS. You need access to the data at low latency and must be highly available. Which of the following would be the ideal data store in AWS?

A. AWS Redshift

B. AWS DynamoDB

C. AWS Aurora

D. AWS S3

Answer: B

Explanation: Amazon DynamoDB is a fully managed NoSQL database service that offers fast and predictable scalability and performance. DynamoDB helps you to load and scale a distributed server so that you do not have to think about installing, setting up and configuring hardware, repeating, patching code or cluster scaling. It is the best place to store data that is in JSON format.

214. Two companies are using the same infrastructure on the AWS Cloud. At first, the web application servers deployed in each VPC would be shared. You intend to configure the VPC between two IT companies as a SysOps company administrator. How is the configuration of routing between peering VPC done to create connectivity between webservers?

A. Each VPC owner should manually add route pointing to CIDR of other VPC

B. Owner of Acceptor VPC will need to do routing for both peering VPC

C. Once VPC peering connection is accepted by acceptor VPC, routes are automatically added in the routing table for each VPC

D. Owner of Requestor VPC will need to do routing for both peering VPC

Answer: A

Explanation: To setup the VPC peering, the VPC holder must send a VPC peering request to the VPC accepter. Once a peering link is established, each VPC holder can attach routes for target servers manually in another VPC pointing to pcx-111222.

215.   You are using AWS S3 bucket to store files and CloudFront distribution for content distribution among the users. The response to the CloudFront requests includes a range of 4xx errors. What is the reason behind these errors? (Choose 2)

A. There is an Internal server error
B. The CloudFront service is unavailable
C. The user does not have access to the underlying bucket
D. The object that the user is requesting for is not present

Answer: C and D

Explanation: The following may be the reason behind the error:

404	Not Found
405	Method Not Allowed
414	Request-URI Too Large
400	Bad Request
403	Forbidden
412	Precondition Failed
415	Unsupported Media Type

216.   A high value for the "SpilloverCount" can be seen from the CloudWatch metrics. In order to ensure that this metric is monitored first as so it does not increase, which of the following should you follow up?

A. CPU Utilization
B. SurgeQueueLength
C. HealthyHostCount
D. BackendConnectionErrors

Answer: B

Explanation: SpilloverCount metric shows the total number of request, which is rejected because of surge queue. When this queue becomes full, the count will start increasing. Monitor SurgeQueueLength metric for avoiding high value in SpilloverCount.

217. You work for a large international corporation as a SysOps administrator. The corporation has a number of critical webservers all over the world. You configured latency-based routing, followed by the weighted routing policy between webservers in different AZs for Web servers in eastern-1 and western-1 regions. These webservers are behind ELB & alias records are created using Route 53 pointing web server domain to this ELB. During failover testing, you are observing that traffic is not shifting to us-west-1 post all instance down in us-east-1 region. What is the reason behind this?

A. Route 53 Health check is missing for US-east-1region
B. Evaluate Target Health check is missing in Alias records for ELB in US-east-1 region
C. Routing Policy is misconfigured. Failover routing should be used instead of weighted routing policy
D. Health Checks for ELB in US-east-1 region is missing

Answer: B

Explanation: A health check monitor is important for all records alias & non-alias in the case of the complex routing policy for Route 53. Route 53 will assume that the missing health check, working & traffic is not diverted to a healthy instance. In the above case, health check evaluation should be enabled for alias records in us-east 1, so when all instances in this region are down, traffic will be shifted to servers in us-west-1.

218. You are using EC2, S3, EFS file system and PostgreSQL and want to encrypt all data at rest without any interruption to the clients. From the following, which will meet the requirement?

A. EFS
B. EBS Volume
C. PostgreSQL
D. S3

Answer: D

Explanation: There are two methods of data encryption at rest: server side encryption and client side encryption. Server side encryption encrypts your data before saving it to S3 while customer side encryption, data is encrypted at the client side and then uploaded to S3.

For other options, you need to recreate it and then enable encryption option that causes interruption to users.

219.   An enterprise hires an external audit to whom they want to give access to logs. In which way would the appropriate access to the auditor be given?

A. By creating an IAM user that has read and write access to the logs created in S3 by CloudTrail

B. By creating Access Keys and giving the Access Keys to the auditor

C. By creating an IAM user that has read access to the logs created in S3 by CloudTrail

D. By creating an IAM Role for the auditor and asking the user to use federated access

Answer: C

Explanation: As the logs are created in S3 by CloudTrail, it logs all the actions taken by user, role or AWS services. So, create an IAM user to whom you give access to Read only to S3 bucket where logs are stored. Then, give credentials of that IAM user to the auditor.

220.   An application is hosted on an EC2 instance that is placed in a subnet. To increase the availability and scalability of the application, what can be done?

A. Create an AutoScaling Group with subnets across 3 availability zones. Set a minimum, desired and maximum capacity as 2

B. Create an AutoScaling Group with subnets across 3 regions. Set a minimum, desired and maximum capacity as 2

C. Create an AutoScaling Group with subnets across 2 availability zones. Set a minimum, desired and maximum capacity as 1

D. Create an AutoScaling Group with subnets across 2 regions. Set a minimum, desired and maximum capacity as 1

Answer: A

Explanation: By using AutoScaling Group, you can take advantage of the reliability of regional redundancy across several Availability Zones with in a region. In case of failure on one AZ, ASG automatically launches the new instance in another AZ. So as per required scenario, you need to use ASG for 3 AZ with minimum and max capacity of 2.

221. There is a collection of EC2 instances. You found that during the analysis of these instances, CPU credits were reduced to zero several times. Which of the following can help to alleviate this? (Choose 2)

A. Use EBS optimized instances
B. Change to a higher instance type
C. Use t1.micro instances
D. Change to t2.unlimited

Answer: B and D

Explanation: An infinite burstable performance example, such as T3 Infinite and T2 Unlimited, can maintain high CPU output for any period of time where appropriate. Where needed. The instance cost for T3 and T2 immediately covers all intermediate fluctuations if the average CPU utilization of the instance happens at or below the baseline over a rolling 24-hour period or the instance lifetime, whichever is shorter. Where the instance is operating at higher CPU use for a longer period, it can do so per vCPU-hour for a flat extra price.

222. An enterprise has an EC2 Instance on which web application is hosted. Currently, the application is facing attacks form the internet. The attacks make use of HTTP requests malformed. What can be used to minimize the attack?

A. AWS WAF
B. Network Access Control Lists
C. AWS AutoScaling Group
D. AWS Application Load Balancer

Answer: A

Explanation: AWS WAF is a web application firewall that helps to safeguard web applications against common web vulnerabilities that can affect the availability, security and inappropriate use of resources in applications. Through specifying customized web security standards, AWS WAF gives you control over which traffic to allow or prevent for your web application. AWS WAF can be used to create specific rules that block common attack methods, such as SQL injection, cross-site scripting, as well as rules designed specifically for your application.

223. An organization is using AWS Glacier to store data from the on-premises Data center. The amount of data is 70TB. When files are uploaded to Glacier, its original name changes to

Archive ID. How could the organization ensure that it has the same file in Glacier in a cost effective way? (Choose 2)

A. By using the AWS Snowball Edge device to upload the files. Here the file names will be the same in Glacier

B. By uploading the files in Amazon S3 Infrequent Access and then using lifecycle policies to move them to Glacier

C. By uploading the files directly to glacier using the AWS Console

D. By using the AWS Snowball to upload the files to S3 and then moving it to Glacier storage for archival using Lifecycle rules

E. By creating a PostGreSQL database and having an entry for files names in Glacier against the action file names

Answer: B and D

Explanation: To save the cost for storing the data with its original name, place it in AWS S3 Infrequent Access and by configuring lifecycle policy, move it to Glacier. You can use Snowball machine for uploading of the files to Amazon S3. The Lifecycle policies can then be used to move the object's storage class to Glacier. Here, the names of the files are maintained.

224. A load balancer and AutoScaling Group are used for the application. The users are facing many 4xx bugs. You should make sure that you understand the customer addresses arising from these mistakes. How can you do this?

A. By getting the logs from the AutoScaling Group

B. The logs would automatically be available. Download the logs using the Elastic Load Balancer Console

C. You can query the client's workstations to get the logs

D. If the Elastic Load Balancer logs were enabled, you could use the logs in the Simple Storage service to get the IP addresses

Answer: D

Explanation: Elastic Load Balancing includes access logs that collect in-depth information on load balancing requests. Every log contains information that includes client IP address, latency paths and server response when the request was sent. This access log is an optional component of Elastic Load balancing, which has been disabled by default. You can use this access logs for analysis of traffic patterns and for trouble shooting. Once access logs for your load balancer are allowed, Elastic Load Balancing collects and stores logs in the Amazon S3 bucket. Access logging can be deactivated at any time.

225. There is a security requirement regarding the logging of API calls for EC2 Instances. All termination API calls to EC2 instances must also be notified as well. How can this specification be automated? (choose any 2)
    A. By creating an SNS topic and adding it as an event destination for the S3 bucket
    B. By creating a Lambda function and adding it as an event destination for the S3 bucket then using SNS topic for notification
    C. By creating a trail in CloudTrail
    D. By creating a log stream in CloudWatch

Answer: B and C

Explanation: AWS CloudTrail is a tool that tracks a client, function or AWS service's behavior. API calls as events can also be recorded by CloudTrail. You build a trail to continuously monitor activities on your AWS account. CloudTrail enables the delivery of activity log files of events to an Amazon S3 bucket. The bucket-notification function of Amazon S3 can be used. Set up Amazon S3 to publish events that are created by objects to AWS Lambda. Each time that CloudTrail enters logs into S3, Amazon S3 can then use the Amazon S3 Object-created Event parameter to invoke your Lambda function. The S3 event contains the bucket name and main name of the log object generated by CloudTrail. You can read the log object in your Lambda function code and process the logged access records from CloudTrail.

226. The AWS VPC has been set up by a company who also launched a new RDS instance of cloud testing services. Now, the company is concerned that the number of instances in a region can exceed the supported RDS instance. Which feature can be allowed to get notified, once the Service Limits reaches to 75 percent of the RDS instance?
    A. Enable Partner-led support plan to create Trusted Advisor checks for RDS instance service limits & create an Amazon CloudWatch alarm based on this check
    B. Enable Enhanced support plan to create Trusted Advisor checks for RDS instance service limits & create an Amazon CloudWatch alarm based on this check
    C. Enable Developer support plan to create Trusted Advisor checks for RDS instance service limits & create an Amazon CloudWatch alarm based on this check
    D. Enable Business support plan to create Trusted Advisor checks for RDS instance service limits & create an Amazon CloudWatch alarm based on this check

Answer: D

Explanation: A CloudWatch Alarm can be generated for service limitations of AWS services with the Business & Enterprise Support Plan. In this scenario, Trusted Advisor checks on the product limits of RDS example using the Business Support Program. With the help of these checks, you can generate a CloudWatch alert that notifies you when the capacity cap is exceeded by 75%.

227. There are configurations that include a private subnet web server and a public subnet bastion host. For the security groups for Bastion host, you set the following Inbound Rules:
    - Protocol Type:TCP
    - >Port Number:22
    - Source:192.168.10.1/32

    - Protocol Type:TCP
    - Port Number:22
    - Source:sg-xxxxxxxx

    - Protocol Type:TCP
    - Port Number:389
    - Source:10.2.1.0/24

Ideally, only the IP address of 192.168.10.1 should be used to connect to the bastion host. But you can see from the logs that there are other IPs that can also bind itself to a bastion host. What is a clear explanation for this in the following?
    A. By default, all IP addresses are allowed communication into the subnet from the internet
    B. The IP addresses belonging to the security group of sg-xxxxxxxx are able to connect to the bastion host
    C. Since you have allowed the connection to port 389, which is higher than port 22, other IPs are also able to establish communications
    D. The source IP of 192.168.10.1/32 does not limit the access to just one IP address

Answer: B

Explanation: Since the bastion host security group also allows communication from the sg-xxxxxx, the IP addresses of this security group can also communicate with the bastion host.

228. What can you do to monitor the memory utilization of EC2 instances?

A. Install scripts on the EC2 Instance to publish custom metrics to CloudWatch
B. Use the AWS Inspector service to configure the Memory utilization of the Instance
C. Use the inbuilt metrics available in CloudWatch
D. Use the AWS Config service to configure the Memory utilization of the Instance

Answer: A

Explanation: For monitoring of memory utilization, you need a custom script that should be installed in an EC2 instance then published to the metric in CloudWatch.

229. Custom metrics are currently published using the AWS CLI. These metrics must be viewed on the dashboard in CloudWatch. How would you do this?
   A. By choosing the desired widget and the inbuilt metric from the custom namespace for that widget
   B. By creating a text widget and choosing the inbuilt metric from the custom namespace for that widget
   C. By choosing the desired widget and the custom metric from the custom namespace for that widget
   D. By creating a text widget and choosing the custom metric from the custom namespace for that widget

Answer: C

Explanation: In CloudWatch, you have an option to choose the desired widget. Here, you must choose the custom metrics that you want to see in the Dashboard.

230. When MFA delete is enabled on S3 bucket, then which action cannot be performed without using MFA Delete? (Choose 2)
   A. Permanently deleting an object version
   B. Suspend versioning on the bucket
   C. Enable versioning on the bucket
   D. Listing down the deleted versions in the bucket

Answer: A and B

Explanation: Use MFA delete on a versioned bucket can add another layer of security. Once you have done so, you must provide access keys to your AWS account and a valid code from the MFA

program of the account to disable or re-activate the bucket versioning and deletion of object permanently.

231. An enterprise has a large number of employees; each employee has its own AWS account. Now the enterprise wants to manage the billing and global permission of all the accounts. What should be used for this?
    A. AWS Consolidated Billing
    B. AWS IAM users
    C. AWS IAM policies
    D. AWS Organization

Answer: D

Explanation: AWS Organizations offers multiple AWS account policy-based management. You may create account groups, automate the account creation, implement and maintain the policies of such groups with AWS Organizations. Organizations centralize the management of policies across multiple accounts without the need for custom scripts or manual processes.

232. An application is using to provide software patches to the client, and the app is hosted in EC2 instance. When users are downloading patches, they face a slow response. What can you use to resolve this issue in a cost effective and efficient way?
    A. Classic Elastic Load Balancer
    B. Route 53
    C. Cloud Front Distribution
    D. Application Elastic Load Balancer

Answer: C

Explanation: Amazon CloudFront is a web service to speed up the delivery of your static, dynamic web content to your customers, like.html,.css,.js and photo files. CloudFront offers the content via a worldwide data center network called edge locations. If a user requests CloudFront content, the client is redirected to the edge of the network with the lowest latency (time delay) to deliver the best possible content.

233. A company uses S3 to store its critical data and is concerned about the attack on these files. The company wants to protect the data from being stolen and subjected to ransomware. How would this be done?
   A. By enabling Versioning on the S3 bucket
   B. By moving the objects to S3-Infrequent Access
   C. By enabling S3 Bucket Encryption
   D. By moving the objects to Amazon Glacier

Answer: A

Explanation: As enabling versions of the AWS, S3 bucket helps preserve and restore S3-modified or removed objects that can assist with malware and accidents.

234. An enterprise wants to shifts its MySQL database from on-premises infrastructure to AWS. How as a SysOps Administrator can you do this in an easy way?
   A. AWS EMR
   B. AWS Redshift
   C. AWS RDS
   D. AWS DynamoDB

Answer: C

Explanation: The Amazon Relational Databased Service (Amazon RDS) is a web service that enables the setup, operation and scale of a relational cloud database. It provides cost-effective, resizable functionality to a relational standard database in the industry and handles common database management tasks.

235. You allowed DiscReadBytes to evaluate the volume of data read by the application, which is running on an EC2 instance, installed on a VPC private subnet. The next day you observed on CloudWatch Metric that 0 bytes were read all day, even though it was read from the EC2 instance. This instance accessed the internet through a NAT gateway. Which one is the reason why 0 bytes are displayed?
   A. You have enabled only Basic Monitoring that does not cover "DiskReadBytes" metric
   B. No Instance store volume is attached to EC2 instance
   C. No EBS volume is attached to EC2 instance

D. An EC2 instance is a part of private subnet due to which it is unable to send metrics to Amazon CloudWatch

Answer: B

Explanation: The metric for "DiskReadBytes" is used to calculate the byte read from the volume of an instance store. If "DiskReadBytes" for the EC2 instance is allowed that has no instance store volume associated with it, the value is registered as o-bytes, or no metric is sent to Amazon CloudWatch.

236. A company has two sets of EC2 instances. Web layer is hosting on one set and database on the other. In these instances, you must maintain internal communication. The instances should ensure that they do not connect with the internet. Which of the following configurations will meet this requirement?
   A. Public subnets in different regions for the web and database layer
   B. Private subnets in different regions for the web and database layer
   C. Public subnets in different availability zones for the web and database layer
   D. Private subnets in different availability zones for the web and database layer

Answer: D

Explanation: As the company wants the instance to be able to communicate with each other but not from the internet, then it should place the sets of instances in private subnet but in different AZs.

237. The company is looking for a MongoDB server that is used widely by a client. An EC2 instance will host the server. You as SysOps Admin provision the environment. Which EBS Volume would you be using for this requirement?
   A. ColdHDD
   B. Provisioned IOPS
   C. General Purpose SSD
   D. Throughput Optimized HDD

Answer: B

Explanation: Provisioned IOPS is for high throughput and low latency workloads for example, large database workloads, such as MongoDB, Cassandra, Microsoft SQL Server, MySQL, PostgreSQL and Oracle.

238.   You work for a startup company as a SysOps administrator. You intend to launch the Amazon S3 bucket with a static website. You have registered the domain and sub-domains name of the proposed website with Amazon Route 53. During the development of this web content in Amazon S3 bucket, which of the following is true for the S3 bucket name?

A. For both Domains & Sub-Domains, the name of Amazon S3 bucket can be different from the name of record created in Amazon Route 53

B. For Sub-Domain, the name of Amazon S3 bucket should be same as the name of record created in Amazon Route 53. For Domain, no need of having S3 bucket name same as the name of record created in Amazon Route 53

C. For both Domains & Sub-Domains, the name of Amazon S3 bucket should be same as the name of record created in Amazon Route 53

D. For Domain, the name of Amazon S3 bucket should be same as the name of record created in Amazon Route 53. For Sub-Domain, no need of having S3 bucket name same as the name of record created in Amazon Route 53

Answer: C

Explanation: The name of the bucket must be the same as that of the registered domain name while using the static website on the Amazon S3 bucket. If a website includes some subdomains, S3 should also be the same as the name of the subdomain.

239.   AWS Direct Connect is being built between your local data center and a VPC in the us-west region. You want to link your data center in the east region of VPC. You should ensure that the link is low in latency and maximum bandwidth. How can you do this in an economical way?

A. By setting up an AWS Direct connect gateway

B. By using VPC peering

C. By creating an AWS Direct Connect connection between the VPC in the us-east region and the on-premise data center

D. By creating an AWS VPN and managing the connection between the VPC in the us-east region and the on-premise data center

Answer: A

Explanation: To connect your VPCs, use the AWS Direct Connect gateway. You can connect Direct Connect gateway to a transit gateway if you have several VPCs in the same region or to the virtual private gateway A Direct Connect gateway, which is a global resource. The Direct Connect Gateway can be built in any public region and accessed from all other public regions.

240. A company has Dev, Test and Prod environments for which it uses Lambda functions. It needs to identify the instances on which applications are running in these environments. Which of the following options would you use to identify the environment?
   A. Instance Metadata
   B. Memory Utilization
   C. CPU Utilization
   D. Resource Tagging

Answer: D

Explanation: Use tags for resource identification. In this way, you can easily target the resource on which you want to perform actions. You can also easily perform filtering, changing and troubleshooting on these resources. With tagging, you can categorize by owner, purpose, and environment.

241. An enterprise uses S3 bucket to store files. There is a number of employees, some of which accidentally deleted files from bucket. Now, the enterprise wants to secure all objects in the buckets to avoid such type of accidental deletion in future. What can be done to accomplish this?
   A. Enable MFA delete by using an IAM user with administrative privileges and using the AWS Console
   B. Enable MFA delete by using root credentials and the AWS CLI
   C. Enable MFA delete by using root credentials and the AWS Console
   D. Enable MFA delete by using an IAM user with administrative privileges and the AWS CLI

Answer: B

Explanation: MFA delete is only able to work with CLI or API. Even via IAM user, you are unable to enable the delete action on MFA delete. It can only be done via root credentials.

242.   A company hosts its application on the Load balancer and AutoScaling Group that is using a lot of memory. For AutoScaling, which default metric can you use as an application?
  A. Instance Metadata
  B. Memory Utilization
  C. CPU Utilization
  D. Resource Tagging

Answer: C

Explanation: This is a tricky matter now. The question says the demand is resource-intensive. By definition, we can, therefore, conclude that by memory usage, we can scale the instances of the AutoScaling Group. But it also specifies that a built-in metric must be used, so memory usage is not an EC2 built-in CloudWatch metric. Therefore, we should use the CPU utilization metric.

243.   How do you as a SysOps Administrator integrate on-premises asymmetric KMS with AWS service?
  A. By creating an EC2 Instance out of the AMI from the AWS Marketplace
  B. By uploading the customer key from KMS to the on-premises service
  C. By using AWS KMS and integrating this with the on-premises service
  D. By using AWS CloudHSM and integrating this with the on-premises service

Answer: D

Explanation: To integrate on-premises KMS with AWS, you can CloudHSM. It works with both symmetric and asymmetric keys. To generate the asymmetric key, use the genRSAKeyPair command.

244.   A company is using VPC in which it places its webserver instances in public subnet and database server in private subnet. The company checked completely that the database server is inaccessible publically, but observed that the webserver is not able to access the external service. How would this issue be resolved?
  A. By creating an internet gateway, attaching it to the VPC, and modifying the route tables for the subnet for the web server
  B. By ensuring that the web server is placed behind an Elastic Load Balancer
  C. By creating a NAT gateway, attaching it to the VPC and modifying the route tables for the subnet for the web server

D. By ensuring that private IP's are assigned to the web servers for communication

Answer: A

Explanation: As webserver is unable to access the external services, an internet gateway needs to be attached and then the route table need to be modified in order for the webserver to be able to communicate.

245.   You are using an S3 bucket to store critical files. You want to get notified about any malicious activity as your files are accessed by clients. In what way would you put security measures without applying too many restrictions on a bucket for the existing clients?

    A. Placing the following statement in the bucket policy { "Version":"2012-10-17", "Statement":[{ "Sid":"AddPerm", "Effect":"Allow", "Principal": "*", "Action":["s3:GetObject"], "Resource":["arn:aws:s3:::examplebucket/*"] }] }

    B. Enabling versioning for the bucket

    C. Using a bucket policy and placing a DENY statement for the PutObject Action

    D. Using AWS Config to monitor any malicious activity and then using SNS to send notifications to the security department

Answer: D

Explanation: AWS Config is a service that allows you to evaluate, audit and evaluate your AWS resources configuration. With AWS Config, you can continuously monitor and record the AWS resource configurations, and you can automatically evaluate recorded configurations against the desired configurations. Config enables you to review changes to AWS resources configurations and relationships between resource. AWS managed rules are provided by AWS Config that covers a broad range of issues related to security, such as checking that your Amazon Elastic Block Store (Amazon EBS) volumes have been encrypted, tagged properly your assets, and allowed root accounts for MFA.

246.   How you can aggregate the monitoring of CPU utilization of all instances in all regions? (Choose 2)

    A. By ensuring detailed monitoring is enabled for the instances

    B. By ensuring basic monitoring is enabled for the instances

C. By creating a custom dashboard, adding widgets for each region, and aggregating the CPU utilization for all instances in a region to each widget

D. By creating a custom dashboard, aggregating the CPU utilization for all instances and adding it as a widget to the dashboard

Answer: A and C

Explanation: You can aggregate the metrics for AWS resources across multiple resources. But Amazon CloudWatch cannot aggregate data across regions because metrics are completely separate between regions. For example, you can aggregate statistics for your EC2 instances that have detailed monitoring enabled. Instances that use basic monitoring are not included. Therefore, you must enable detailed monitoring (at an additional charge), which provides data in 1-minute periods. Then create a widget for each region in a dashboard that will add all instances to CPU utilization metric in each region.

247. An application is hosting in AWS. The application has been the target of massive DDoS attacks on the last few occasions. As a result, most users complained about the application's slowness. However, if such situations arise in the future, you have to avoid these and need 24* 7 support from AWS. In this respect, which of the following services can help?
A. AWS System Manager
B. AWS WAF
C. AWS Inspector
D. AWS Shield Advance

Answer: D

Explanation: You can subscribe to AWS Shield Advanced for greater protection against attacks targeting your AWS EC2, ELB, CloudFront and AWS Route 53 applications. AWS Shield Advanced also provides additional detection and reduction of massive and complex DDoS attacks, close to real-time visibility of threats and integration with AWS WAF a web-based application firewall, in addition to the network and transportation layer security offered by default. You can also access the AWS DDoS Response Team (DRT) 24x 7 and defend yourself from DDoS spikes in your EC, CloudFront, ELB and Route 53 by using AWS Shield Advanced.

248. An organization has two AWS accounts that have individual VPCs in a different region. Such VPCs have to interact among themselves with non-overlapping CIDR blocks. Which of the following is cost effective solution?

A. NAT Gateway

B. VPC Peering between the 2 VPCs

C. VPN Connections

D. AWS Direct Connect

Answer: B

Explanation: A VPC peering connects two VPCs that allow you to connect private traffic between them. Any VPC instance can interact as if it is on the same network. You may establish a VPC peering link in another AWS or with a VPC in another AWS region from your own VPCs. AWS uses the current VPC infrastructure to make a VPC peering connection; it is not a gateway and does not rely on any separate physical hardware.

249. A company is using EC2 instances that reach 100% CPU utilization. You want to restart the instances after 2 minutes of reaching the threshold. How would you automate this? (Choose 2)

A. By using CloudTrail events to restart the instances

B. By using basic monitoring for the instances

C. By using CloudWatch alarms based on CPU Utilization and choosing the action to restart the instance

D. By using detailed monitoring for the instances

Answer: C and D

Explanation: Amazon EC2 sends metric information in five minutes by default to CloudWatch. You can enable enhanced monitoring for instances that sends metric information to CloudWatch in 1-minute intervals. You can automatically create alarms that perform an action to stop, restart, or restore instances using Amazon CloudWatch alarm. You can use stop-and-termination actions to save money on those that are no longer needed. If there is a device failure, you can use the reset and recover actions to automate the restart and restore of these instances on new hardware.

250. A three tier application is hosted behind an ELB with S3 bucket. The contents are stored in the bucket, and CloudFront is used for caching. The firm plans to use the domain name of its own. Worldwide clients must access internet contents at the lowest latency. What is a cost-effective solution when making Route 53 name records?

A. Creating an Alias record for web application pointing to CloudFront distribution

B. Creating a CNAME record for web application pointing to CloudFront distribution

C. Creating a CNAME record for web application pointing to Amazon S3 bucket with the same name

D. Creating an Alias record for web application pointing to Amazon S3 bucket with the same name

Answer: A

Explanation: To redirect traffic to a specific AWS asset, a record can be generated. Create an Alias record of your own domain and point it to a Cloud Front Distribution. When a user accesses a web application from any area, it will be guided to the nearest edge of CloudFront to find the lowest-latency web content.

251.   An application needs to be hosted on EC2 instances. The application needs to download and install a lot of dependent files and must be accessible on another collection of EC2 instances as quickly as possible. How can you achieve this?

A. By creating an Elastic Beanstalk environment and ensuring the stack downloads the necessary application and files
B. By creating an Opswork stack and ensuring the stack downloads the necessary application and files
C. By creating an AMI with the application and the necessary library files
D. By using the User Data section to install the application and the necessary library files

Answer: C

Explanation: An Amazon Machine Image (AMI) is a tool with which you can launch the instances. AMI provides the information required for launching. You just need to specify the source AMI. With a single AMI, you can launch multiple instances with the same configuration. You can use different AMIs to launch instances when you need instances with different configurations.

AMI includes the template of root volume, launch permission and a block device mapping that specify the volume needed to launch the instance.

About Our Products

Other products from IPSpecialist LTD regarding Cloud technology are:

- AWS Certified Cloud Practitioner version 3 Technology Workbook
- AWS Certified Solutions Architect – Associate version 2 Technology Workbook
- AWS Certified Developer – Associate version 2 Technology Workbook
- AWS Certified SysOps Administrator – Associate version 4 Technology Workbook
- AWS Certified Solutions Architect - Professional Technology Workbook
- AWS Certified DevOps Engineer – Professional Technology Workbook
- AWS Certified Advanced Networking – Specialty Technology Workbook
- AWS Certified Big Data – Specialty Technology Workbook
- AWS Certified Security – Specialty Technology Workbook
- Google Certified Associate Cloud Engineer Technology Workbook
- Google Certified Professional Cloud Architect Technology Workbook

Our Upcoming Books

- DevOps Engineer Professional version 2

Note from the Author:

Reviews are gold to authors! If you have enjoyed this book and it has helped you along your certification, would you consider rating and reviewing it?

Link to Product Page: